THE COMIC BOOK BIBLE
FROM JACOB TO MOSES
Published by Scandinavia Publishing House 2012
Scandinavia Publishing House, Drejervej 15,3, DK-2400 Copenhagen, NV, Denmark
info@scanpublishing.dk
www.scanpublishing.dk

Concept by Jose Perez Montero
Text copyright © Ben Alex
Illustrations copyright © Jose Perez Montero
Design by Ben Alex
Printed in China
Hardcover ISBN 978 87 7132 053 4
Softcover ISBN 978 87 7132 052 7
All rights reserved

THE COMIC BOOK BIBLE

FROM JACOB TO MOSES

CONCEPT AND ILLUSTRATIONS BY
JOSE PEREZ MONTERO

TEXT BY BEN ALEX

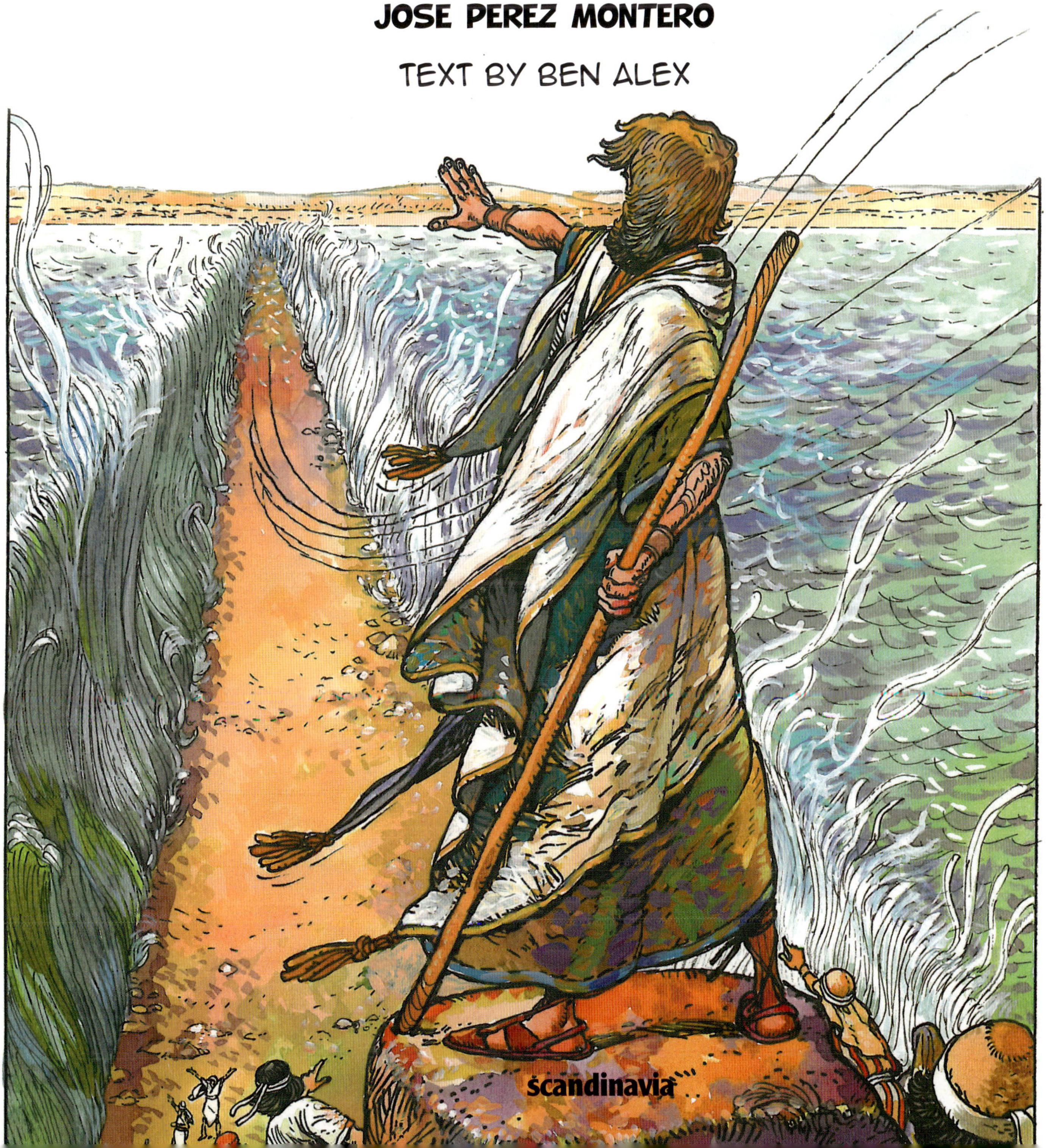

scandinavia

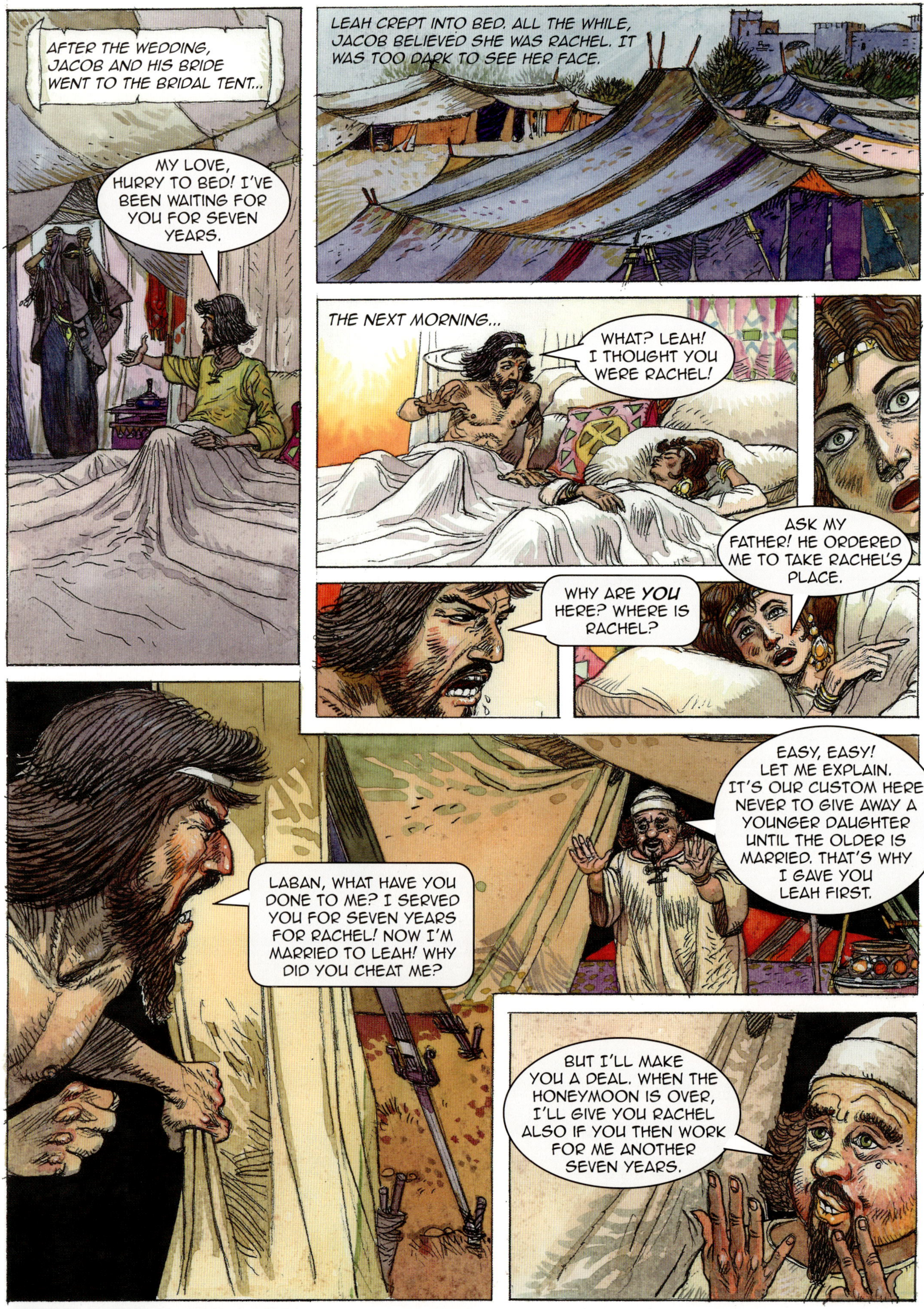

AFTER THE WEDDING, JACOB AND HIS BRIDE WENT TO THE BRIDAL TENT...
MY LOVE, HURRY TO BED! I'VE BEEN WAITING FOR YOU FOR SEVEN YEARS.
LEAH CREPT INTO BED. ALL THE WHILE, JACOB BELIEVED SHE WAS RACHEL. IT WAS TOO DARK TO SEE HER FACE.
THE NEXT MORNING...
WHAT? LEAH! I THOUGHT YOU WERE RACHEL!
WHY ARE YOU HERE? WHERE IS RACHEL?
ASK MY FATHER! HE ORDERED ME TO TAKE RACHEL'S PLACE.
LABAN, WHAT HAVE YOU DONE TO ME? I SERVED YOU FOR SEVEN YEARS FOR RACHEL! NOW I'M MARRIED TO LEAH! WHY DID YOU CHEAT ME?
EASY, EASY! LET ME EXPLAIN. IT'S OUR CUSTOM HERE NEVER TO GIVE AWAY A YOUNGER DAUGHTER UNTIL THE OLDER IS MARRIED. THAT'S WHY I GAVE YOU LEAH FIRST.
BUT I'LL MAKE YOU A DEAL. WHEN THE HONEYMOON IS OVER, I'LL GIVE YOU RACHEL ALSO IF YOU THEN WORK FOR ME ANOTHER SEVEN YEARS.

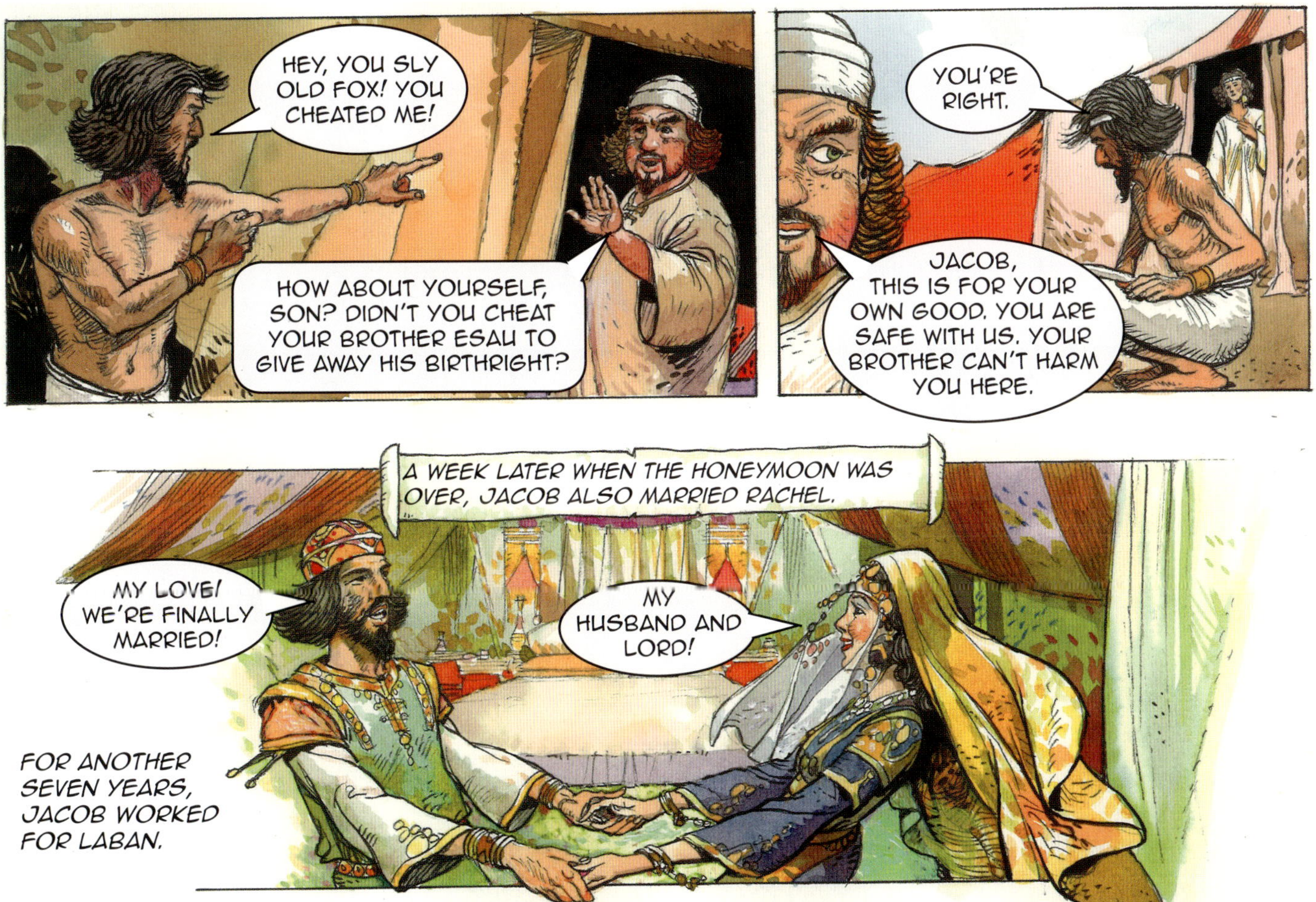
HEY, YOU SLY OLD FOX! YOU CHEATED ME!
HOW ABOUT YOURSELF, SON? DIDN'T YOU CHEAT YOUR BROTHER ESAU TO GIVE AWAY HIS BIRTHRIGHT?
YOU'RE RIGHT.
JACOB, THIS IS FOR YOUR OWN GOOD. YOU ARE SAFE WITH US. YOUR BROTHER CAN'T HARM YOU HERE.
A WEEK LATER WHEN THE HONEYMOON WAS OVER, JACOB ALSO MARRIED RACHEL.
MY LOVE! WE'RE FINALLY MARRIED!
MY HUSBAND AND LORD!
FOR ANOTHER SEVEN YEARS, JACOB WORKED FOR LABAN.

LEAH FELT SAD THAT JACOB DIDN'T LOVE HER THE SAME WAY HE LOVED HER SISTER RACHEL. BUT GOD SHOWED MERCY ON LEAH. HE GAVE HER FOUR SONS -- REUBEN, SIMEON, LEVI, AND JUDAH. RACHEL HAD NO CHILDREN AT ALL.

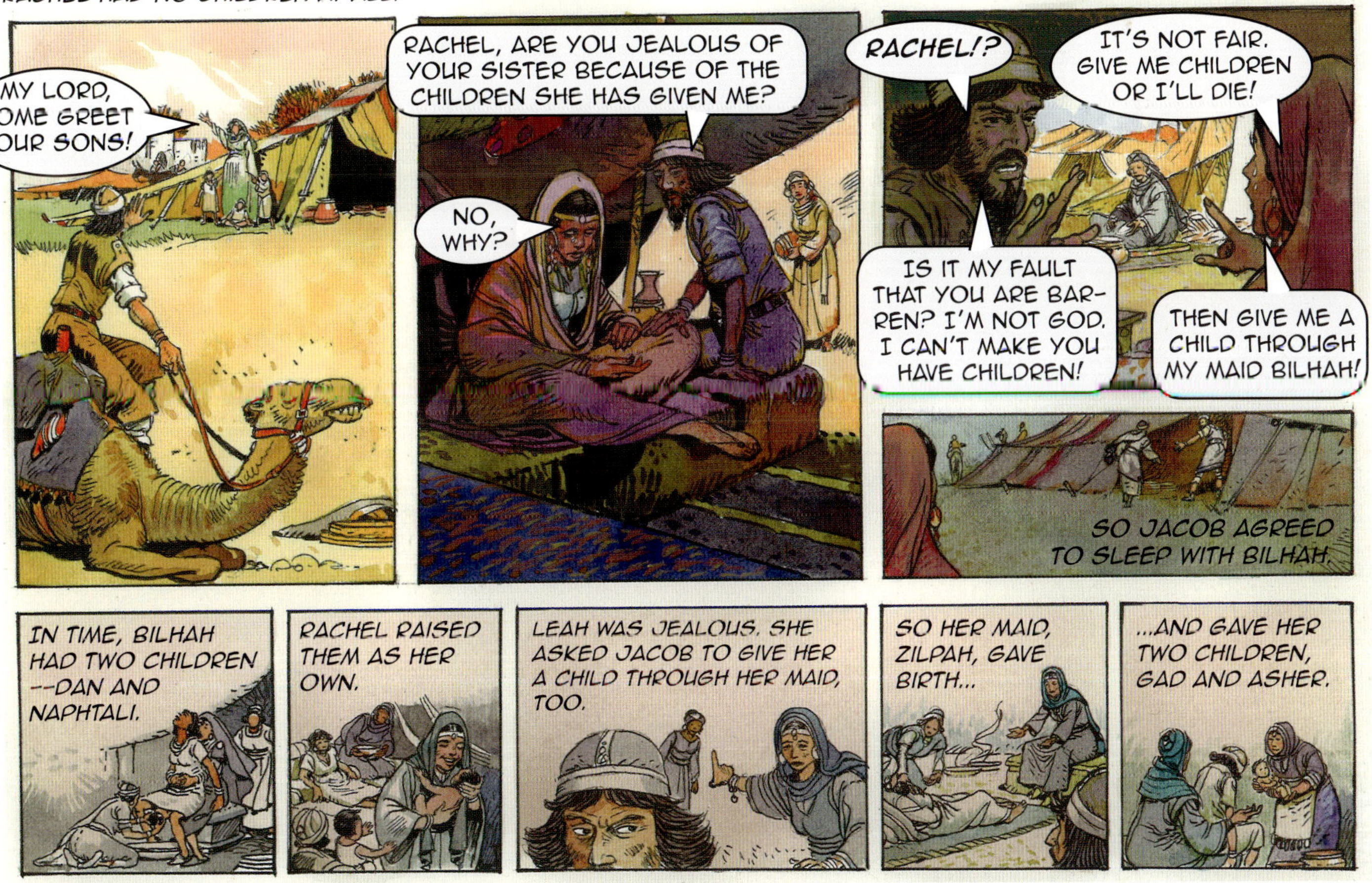
MY LORD, COME GREET YOUR SONS!
RACHEL, ARE YOU JEALOUS OF YOUR SISTER BECAUSE OF THE CHILDREN SHE HAS GIVEN ME?
NO, WHY?
RACHEL!?
IT'S NOT FAIR. GIVE ME CHILDREN OR I'LL DIE!
IS IT MY FAULT THAT YOU ARE BARREN? I'M NOT GOD. I CAN'T MAKE YOU HAVE CHILDREN!
THEN GIVE ME A CHILD THROUGH MY MAID BILHAH!
SO JACOB AGREED TO SLEEP WITH BILHAH.
IN TIME, BILHAH HAD TWO CHILDREN --DAN AND NAPHTALI.
RACHEL RAISED THEM AS HER OWN.
LEAH WAS JEALOUS. SHE ASKED JACOB TO GIVE HER A CHILD THROUGH HER MAID, TOO.
SO HER MAID, ZILPAH, GAVE BIRTH...
...AND GAVE HER TWO CHILDREN, GAD AND ASHER.

RACHEL AND LEAH THOUGHT JACOB WOULD LOVE THEM ACCORDING TO HOW MANY CHILDREN THEY GAVE HIM.

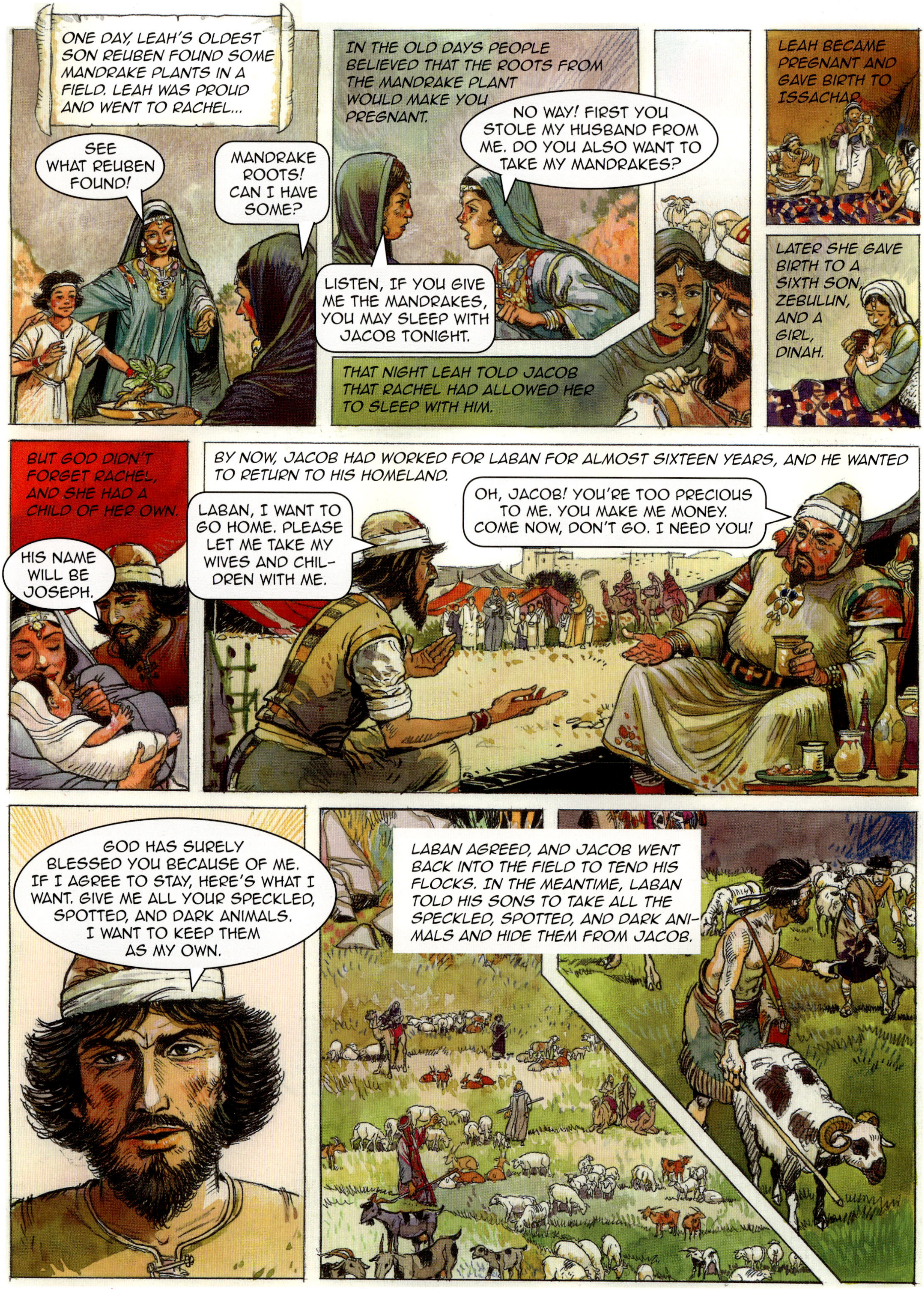
ONE DAY, LEAH'S OLDEST SON REUBEN FOUND SOME MANDRAKE PLANTS IN A FIELD. LEAH WAS PROUD AND WENT TO RACHEL...
SEE WHAT REUBEN FOUND!
MANDRAKE ROOTS! CAN I HAVE SOME?
IN THE OLD DAYS PEOPLE BELIEVED THAT THE ROOTS FROM THE MANDRAKE PLANT WOULD MAKE YOU PREGNANT.
NO WAY! FIRST YOU STOLE MY HUSBAND FROM ME. DO YOU ALSO WANT TO TAKE MY MANDRAKES?
LISTEN, IF YOU GIVE ME THE MANDRAKES, YOU MAY SLEEP WITH JACOB TONIGHT.
THAT NIGHT LEAH TOLD JACOB THAT RACHEL HAD ALLOWED HER TO SLEEP WITH HIM.
LEAH BECAME PREGNANT AND GAVE BIRTH TO ISSACHAR.
LATER SHE GAVE BIRTH TO A SIXTH SON, ZEBULUN, AND A GIRL, DINAH.
BUT GOD DIDN'T FORGET RACHEL, AND SHE HAD A CHILD OF HER OWN.
HIS NAME WILL BE JOSEPH.
BY NOW, JACOB HAD WORKED FOR LABAN FOR ALMOST SIXTEEN YEARS, AND HE WANTED TO RETURN TO HIS HOMELAND.
LABAN, I WANT TO GO HOME. PLEASE LET ME TAKE MY WIVES AND CHILDREN WITH ME.
OH, JACOB! YOU'RE TOO PRECIOUS TO ME. YOU MAKE ME MONEY. COME NOW, DON'T GO. I NEED YOU!
GOD HAS SURELY BLESSED YOU BECAUSE OF ME. IF I AGREE TO STAY, HERE'S WHAT I WANT. GIVE ME ALL YOUR SPECKLED, SPOTTED, AND DARK ANIMALS. I WANT TO KEEP THEM AS MY OWN.
LABAN AGREED, AND JACOB WENT BACK INTO THE FIELD TO TEND HIS FLOCKS. IN THE MEANTIME, LABAN TOLD HIS SONS TO TAKE ALL THE SPECKLED, SPOTTED, AND DARK ANIMALS AND HIDE THEM FROM JACOB.

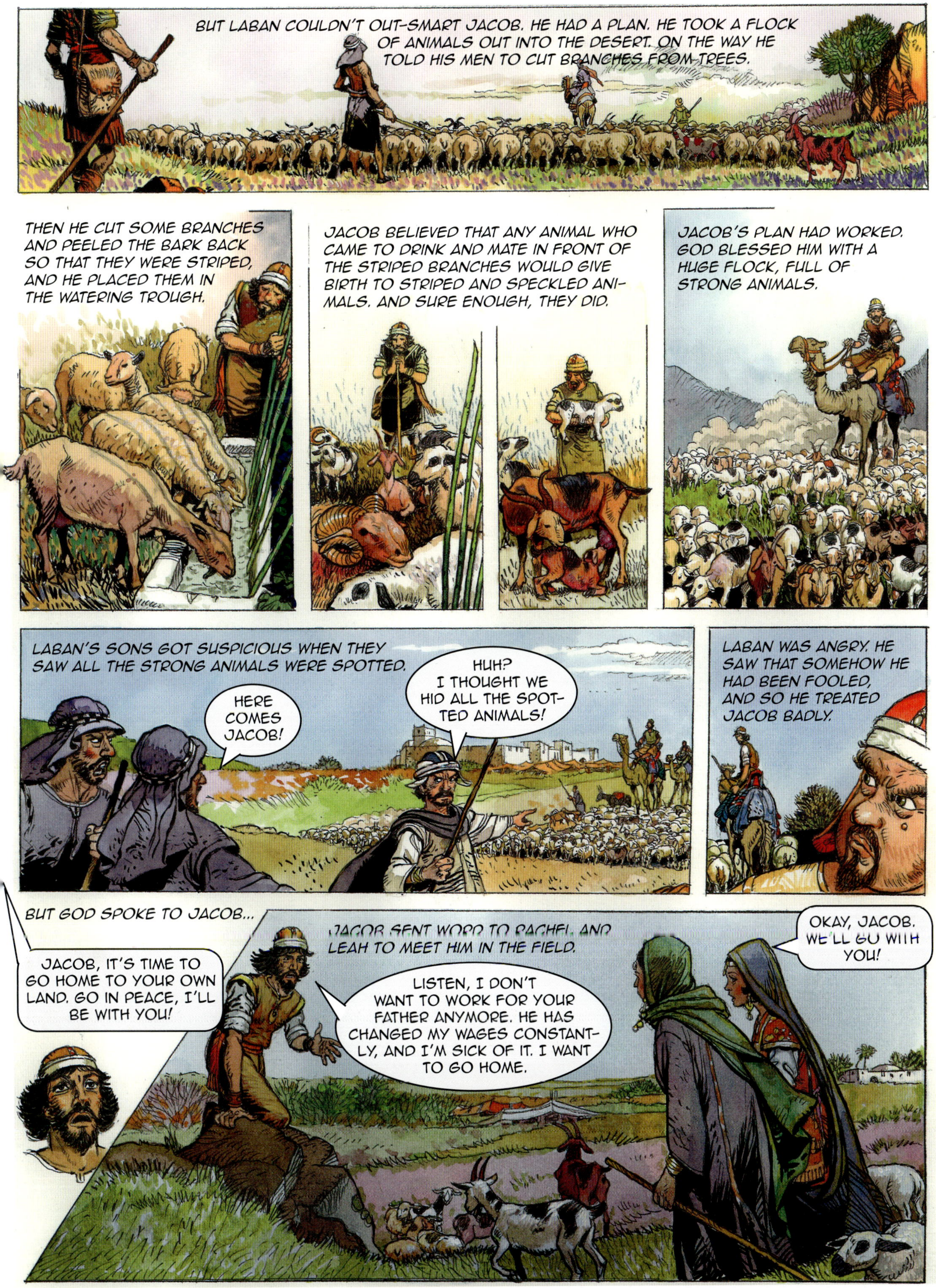

BUT LABAN COULDN'T OUT-SMART JACOB. HE HAD A PLAN. HE TOOK A FLOCK OF ANIMALS OUT INTO THE DESERT. ON THE WAY HE TOLD HIS MEN TO CUT BRANCHES FROM TREES.
THEN HE CUT SOME BRANCHES AND PEELED THE BARK BACK SO THAT THEY WERE STRIPED, AND HE PLACED THEM IN THE WATERING TROUGH.
JACOB BELIEVED THAT ANY ANIMAL WHO CAME TO DRINK AND MATE IN FRONT OF THE STRIPED BRANCHES WOULD GIVE BIRTH TO STRIPED AND SPECKLED ANIMALS. AND SURE ENOUGH, THEY DID.
JACOB'S PLAN HAD WORKED. GOD BLESSED HIM WITH A HUGE FLOCK, FULL OF STRONG ANIMALS.
LABAN'S SONS GOT SUSPICIOUS WHEN THEY SAW ALL THE STRONG ANIMALS WERE SPOTTED.
HERE COMES JACOB!
HUH? I THOUGHT WE HID ALL THE SPOTTED ANIMALS!
LABAN WAS ANGRY. HE SAW THAT SOMEHOW HE HAD BEEN FOOLED, AND SO HE TREATED JACOB BADLY.
BUT GOD SPOKE TO JACOB...
JACOB, IT'S TIME TO GO HOME TO YOUR OWN LAND. GO IN PEACE, I'LL BE WITH YOU!
JACOB SENT WORD TO RACHEL AND LEAH TO MEET HIM IN THE FIELD.
LISTEN, I DON'T WANT TO WORK FOR YOUR FATHER ANYMORE. HE HAS CHANGED MY WAGES CONSTANTLY, AND I'M SICK OF IT. I WANT TO GO HOME.
OKAY, JACOB. WE'LL GO WITH YOU!

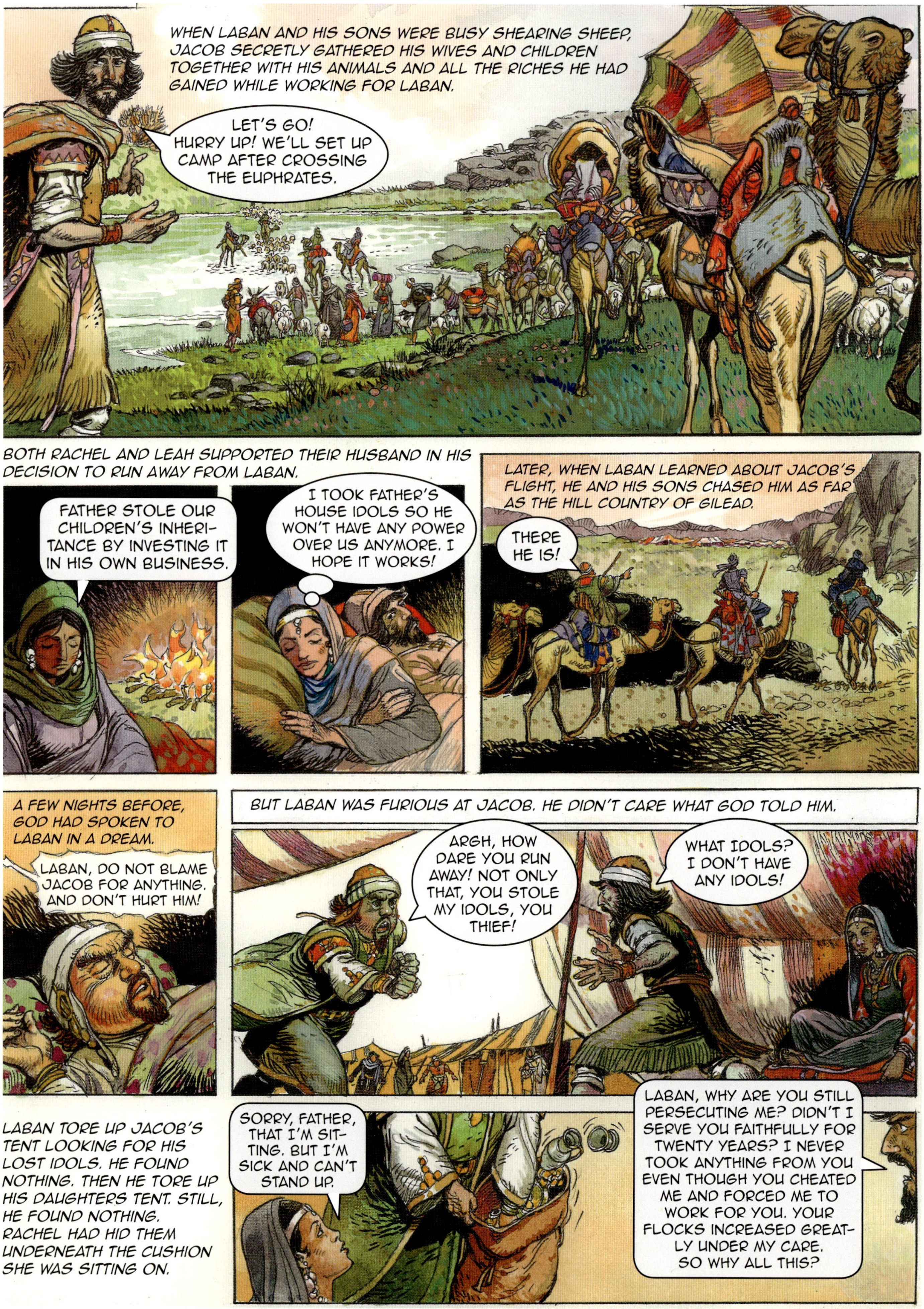

WHEN LABAN AND HIS SONS WERE BUSY SHEARING SHEEP, JACOB SECRETLY GATHERED HIS WIVES AND CHILDREN TOGETHER WITH HIS ANIMALS AND ALL THE RICHES HE HAD GAINED WHILE WORKING FOR LABAN.
LET'S GO! HURRY UP! WE'LL SET UP CAMP AFTER CROSSING THE EUPHRATES.
BOTH RACHEL AND LEAH SUPPORTED THEIR HUSBAND IN HIS DECISION TO RUN AWAY FROM LABAN.
FATHER STOLE OUR CHILDREN'S INHERI-TANCE BY INVESTING IT IN HIS OWN BUSINESS.
I TOOK FATHER'S HOUSE IDOLS SO HE WON'T HAVE ANY POWER OVER US ANYMORE. I HOPE IT WORKS!
LATER, WHEN LABAN LEARNED ABOUT JACOB'S FLIGHT, HE AND HIS SONS CHASED HIM AS FAR AS THE HILL COUNTRY OF GILEAD.
THERE HE IS!
A FEW NIGHTS BEFORE, GOD HAD SPOKEN TO LABAN IN A DREAM.
LABAN, DO NOT BLAME JACOB FOR ANYTHING. AND DON'T HURT HIM!
BUT LABAN WAS FURIOUS AT JACOB. HE DIDN'T CARE WHAT GOD TOLD HIM.
ARGH, HOW DARE YOU RUN AWAY! NOT ONLY THAT, YOU STOLE MY IDOLS, YOU THIEF!
WHAT IDOLS? I DON'T HAVE ANY IDOLS!
LABAN TORE UP JACOB'S TENT LOOKING FOR HIS LOST IDOLS. HE FOUND NOTHING. THEN HE TORE UP HIS DAUGHTERS TENT. STILL, HE FOUND NOTHING. RACHEL HAD HID THEM UNDERNEATH THE CUSHION SHE WAS SITTING ON.
SORRY, FATHER, THAT I'M SIT-TING. BUT I'M SICK AND CAN'T STAND UP.
LABAN, WHY ARE YOU STILL PERSECUTING ME? DIDN'T I SERVE YOU FAITHFULLY FOR TWENTY YEARS? I NEVER TOOK ANYTHING FROM YOU EVEN THOUGH YOU CHEATED ME AND FORCED ME TO WORK FOR YOU. YOUR FLOCKS INCREASED GREAT-LY UNDER MY CARE. SO WHY ALL THIS?

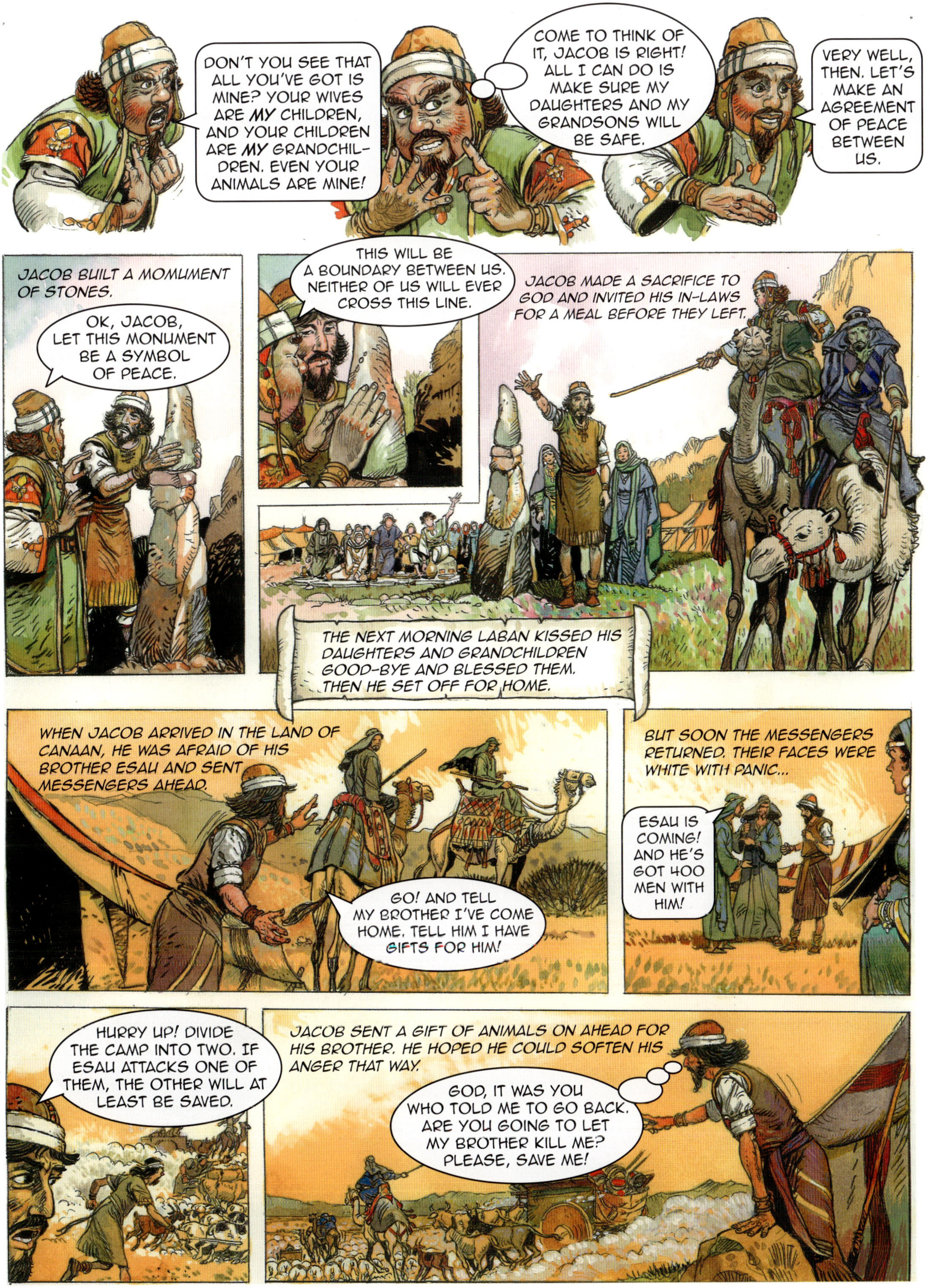
DON'T YOU SEE THAT ALL YOU'VE GOT IS MINE? YOUR WIVES ARE MY CHILDREN, AND YOUR CHILDREN ARE MY GRANDCHIL-DREN. EVEN YOUR ANIMALS ARE MINE!
COME TO THINK OF IT, JACOB IS RIGHT! ALL I CAN DO IS MAKE SURE MY DAUGHTERS AND MY GRANDSONS WILL BE SAFE.
VERY WELL, THEN. LET'S MAKE AN AGREEMENT OF PEACE BETWEEN US.
JACOB BUILT A MOMUMENT OF STONES.
OK, JACOB, LET THIS MONUMENT BE A SYMBOL OF PEACE.
THIS WILL BE A BOUNDARY BETWEEN US. NEITHER OF US WILL EVER CROSS THIS LINE.
JACOB MADE A SACRIFICE TO GOD AND INVITED HIS IN-LAWS FOR A MEAL BEFORE THEY LEFT.
THE NEXT MORNING LABAN KISSED HIS DAUGHTERS AND GRANDCHILDREN GOOD-BYE AND BLESSED THEM. THEN HE SET OFF FOR HOME.
WHEN JACOB ARRIVED IN THE LAND OF CANAAN, HE WAS AFRAID OF HIS BROTHER ESAU AND SENT MESSENGERS AHEAD.
GO! AND TELL MY BROTHER I'VE COME HOME. TELL HIM I HAVE GIFTS FOR HIM!
BUT SOON THE MESSENGERS RETURNED. THEIR FACES WERE WHITE WITH PANIC...
ESAU IS COMING! AND HE'S GOT 400 MEN WITH HIM!
HURRY UP! DIVIDE THE CAMP INTO TWO. IF ESAU ATTACKS ONE OF THEM, THE OTHER WILL AT LEAST BE SAVED.
JACOB SENT A GIFT OF ANIMALS ON AHEAD FOR HIS BROTHER. HE HOPED HE COULD SOFTEN HIS ANGER THAT WAY.
GOD, IT WAS YOU WHO TOLD ME TO GO BACK. ARE YOU GOING TO LET MY BROTHER KILL ME? PLEASE, SAVE ME!

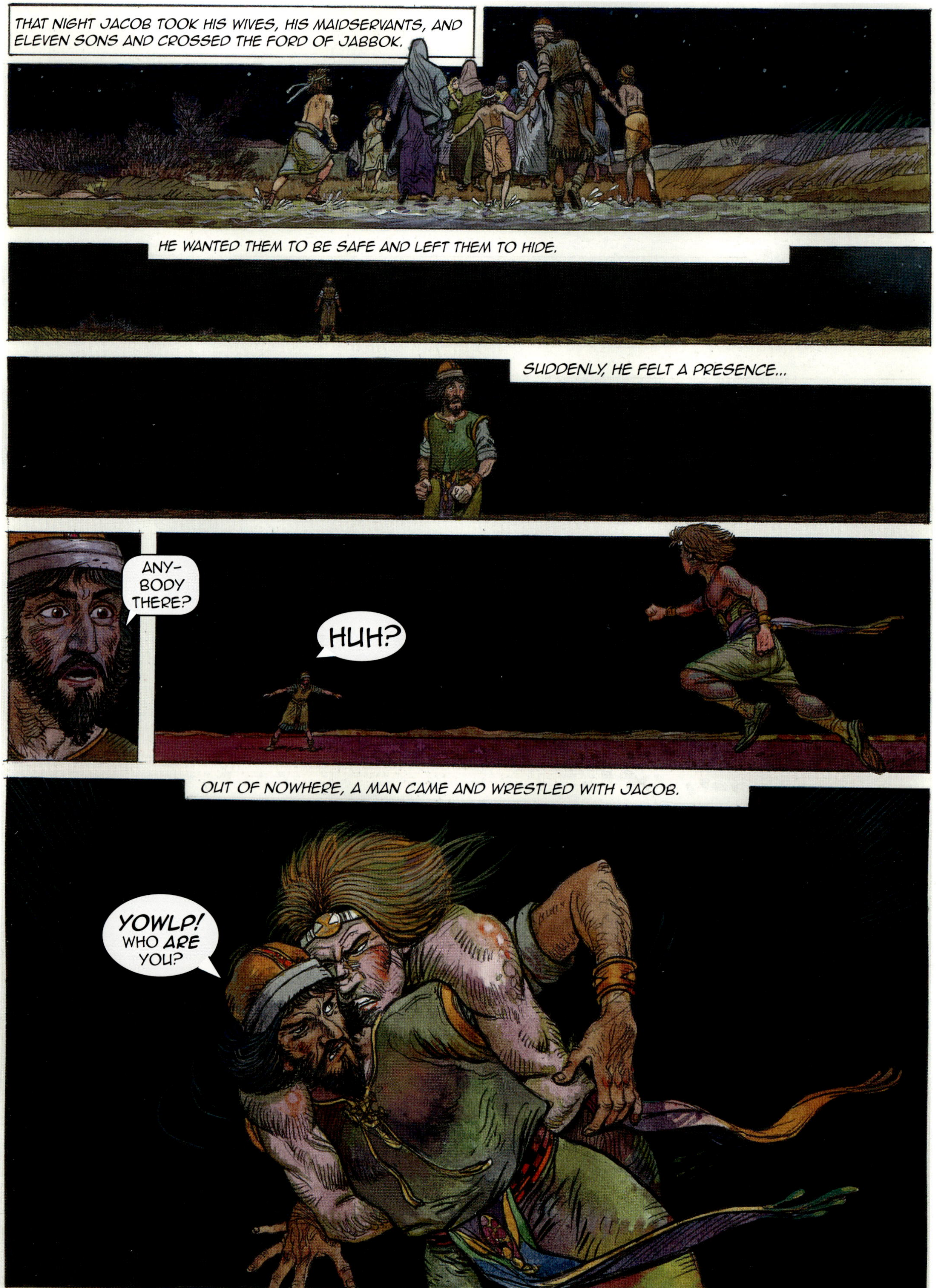
THAT NIGHT JACOB TOOK HIS WIVES, HIS MAIDSERVANTS, AND ELEVEN SONS AND CROSSED THE FORD OF JABBOK.
HE WANTED THEM TO BE SAFE AND LEFT THEM TO HIDE.
SUDDENLY, HE FELT A PRESENCE...
ANY-BODY THERE?
HUH?
OUT OF NOWHERE, A MAN CAME AND WRESTLED WITH JACOB.
YOWLP! WHO ARE YOU?

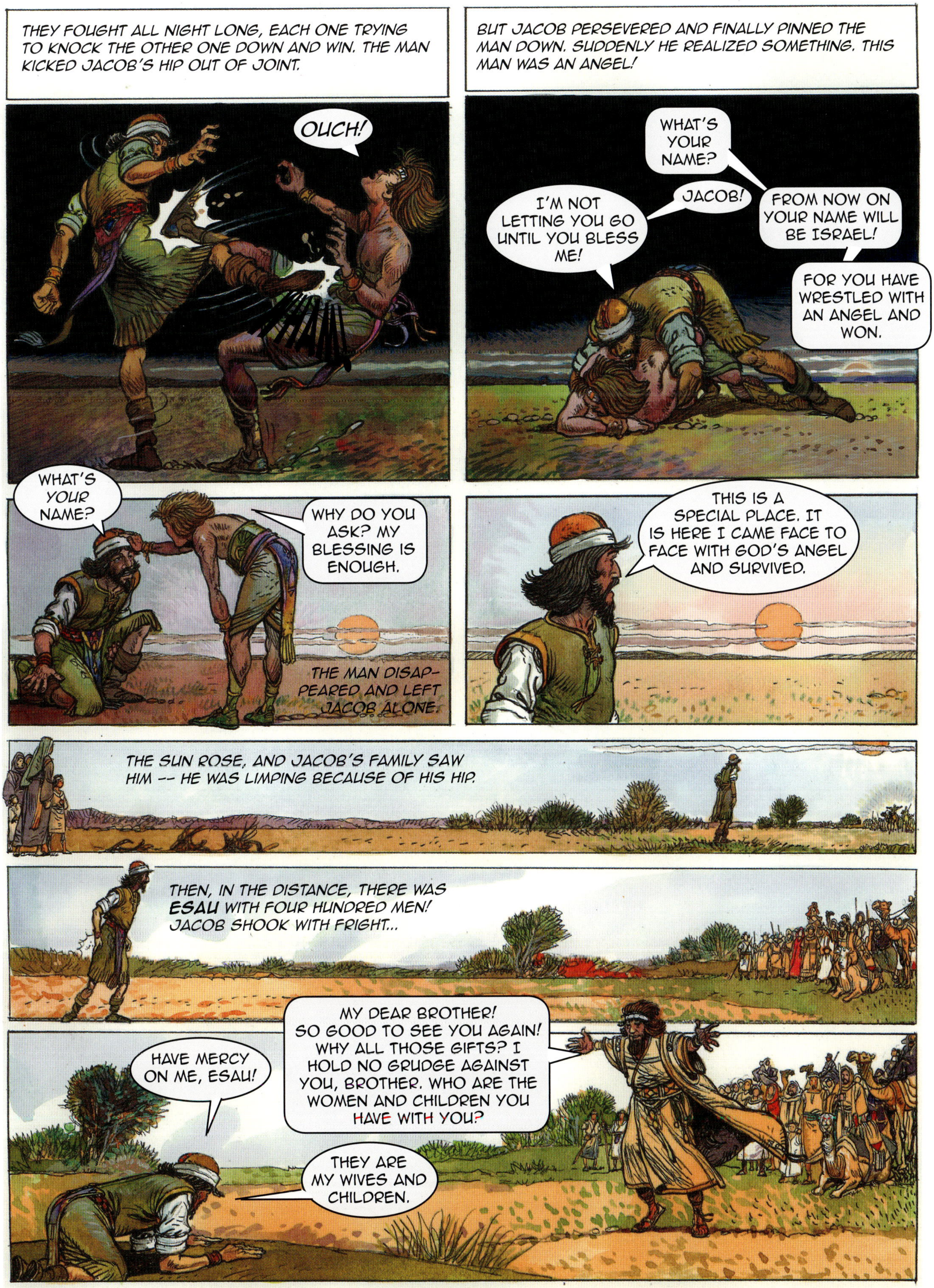

THEY FOUGHT ALL NIGHT LONG, EACH ONE TRYING TO KNOCK THE OTHER ONE DOWN AND WIN. THE MAN KICKED JACOB'S HIP OUT OF JOINT.
OUCH!
BUT JACOB PERSEVERED AND FINALLY PINNED THE MAN DOWN. SUDDENLY HE REALIZED SOMETHING. THIS MAN WAS AN ANGEL!
WHAT'S YOUR NAME?
I'M NOT LETTING YOU GO UNTIL YOU BLESS ME!
JACOB!
FROM NOW ON YOUR NAME WILL BE ISRAEL!
FOR YOU HAVE WRESTLED WITH AN ANGEL AND WON.
WHAT'S YOUR NAME?
WHY DO YOU ASK? MY BLESSING IS ENOUGH.
THE MAN DISAPPEARED AND LEFT JACOB ALONE.
THIS IS A SPECIAL PLACE. IT IS HERE I CAME FACE TO FACE WITH GOD'S ANGEL AND SURVIVED.
THE SUN ROSE, AND JACOB'S FAMILY SAW HIM -- HE WAS LIMPING BECAUSE OF HIS HIP.
THEN, IN THE DISTANCE, THERE WAS ESAU WITH FOUR HUNDRED MEN! JACOB SHOOK WITH FRIGHT...
HAVE MERCY ON ME, ESAU!
MY DEAR BROTHER! SO GOOD TO SEE YOU AGAIN! WHY ALL THOSE GIFTS? I HOLD NO GRUDGE AGAINST YOU, BROTHER. WHO ARE THE WOMEN AND CHILDREN YOU HAVE WITH YOU?
THEY ARE MY WIVES AND CHILDREN.

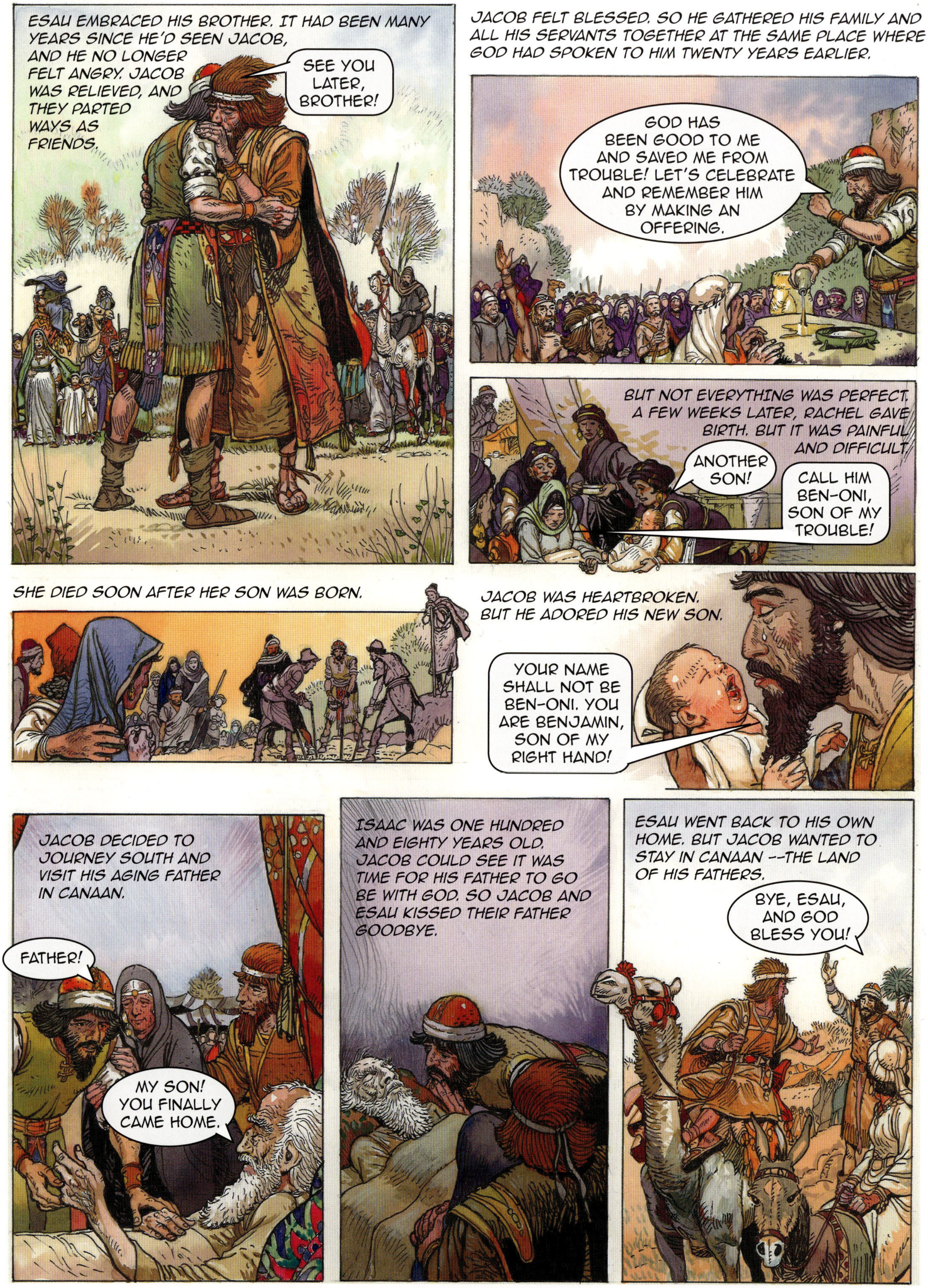
ESAU EMBRACED HIS BROTHER. IT HAD BEEN MANY YEARS SINCE HE'D SEEN JACOB, AND HE NO LONGER FELT ANGRY. JACOB WAS RELIEVED, AND THEY PARTED WAYS AS FRIENDS.
SEE YOU LATER, BROTHER!
JACOB FELT BLESSED. SO HE GATHERED HIS FAMILY AND ALL HIS SERVANTS TOGETHER AT THE SAME PLACE WHERE GOD HAD SPOKEN TO HIM TWENTY YEARS EARLIER.
GOD HAS BEEN GOOD TO ME AND SAVED ME FROM TROUBLE! LET'S CELEBRATE AND REMEMBER HIM BY MAKING AN OFFERING.
BUT NOT EVERYTHING WAS PERFECT. A FEW WEEKS LATER, RACHEL GAVE BIRTH. BUT IT WAS PAINFUL AND DIFFICULT.
ANOTHER SON!
CALL HIM BEN-ONI, SON OF MY TROUBLE!
SHE DIED SOON AFTER HER SON WAS BORN.
JACOB WAS HEARTBROKEN. BUT HE ADORED HIS NEW SON.
YOUR NAME SHALL NOT BE BEN-ONI. YOU ARE BENJAMIN, SON OF MY RIGHT HAND!
JACOB DECIDED TO JOURNEY SOUTH AND VISIT HIS AGING FATHER IN CANAAN.
FATHER!
MY SON! YOU FINALLY CAME HOME.
ISAAC WAS ONE HUNDRED AND EIGHTY YEARS OLD. JACOB COULD SEE IT WAS TIME FOR HIS FATHER TO GO BE WITH GOD. SO JACOB AND ESAU KISSED THEIR FATHER GOODBYE.
ESAU WENT BACK TO HIS OWN HOME. BUT JACOB WANTED TO STAY IN CANAAN --THE LAND OF HIS FATHERS.
BYE, ESAU, AND GOD BLESS YOU!

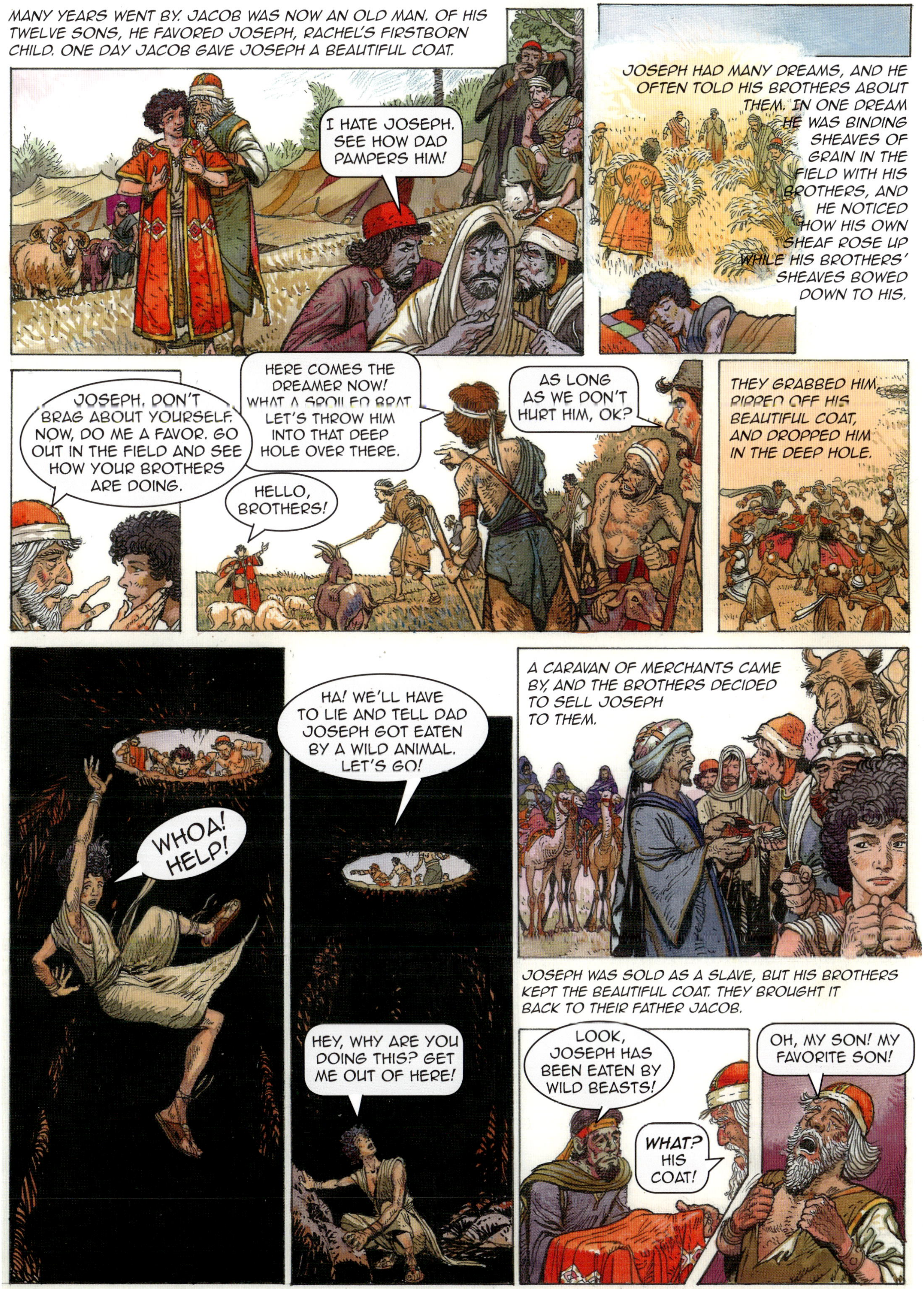
MANY YEARS WENT BY. JACOB WAS NOW AN OLD MAN. OF HIS TWELVE SONS, HE FAVORED JOSEPH, RACHEL'S FIRSTBORN CHILD. ONE DAY JACOB GAVE JOSEPH A BEAUTIFUL COAT.
I HATE JOSEPH. SEE HOW DAD PAMPERS HIM!
JOSEPH HAD MANY DREAMS, AND HE OFTEN TOLD HIS BROTHERS ABOUT THEM. IN ONE DREAM HE WAS BINDING SHEAVES OF GRAIN IN THE FIELD WITH HIS BROTHERS, AND HE NOTICED HOW HIS OWN SHEAF ROSE UP WHILE HIS BROTHERS' SHEAVES BOWED DOWN TO HIS.
JOSEPH, DON'T BRAG ABOUT YOURSELF. NOW, DO ME A FAVOR. GO OUT IN THE FIELD AND SEE HOW YOUR BROTHERS ARE DOING.
HELLO, BROTHERS!
HERE COMES THE DREAMER NOW! WHAT A SPOILED BRAT. LET'S THROW HIM INTO THAT DEEP HOLE OVER THERE.
AS LONG AS WE DON'T HURT HIM, OK?
THEY GRABBED HIM, RIPPED OFF HIS BEAUTIFUL COAT, AND DROPPED HIM IN THE DEEP HOLE.
WHOA! HELP!
HA! WE'LL HAVE TO LIE AND TELL DAD JOSEPH GOT EATEN BY A WILD ANIMAL. LET'S GO!
HEY, WHY ARE YOU DOING THIS? GET ME OUT OF HERE!
A CARAVAN OF MERCHANTS CAME BY, AND THE BROTHERS DECIDED TO SELL JOSEPH TO THEM.
JOSEPH WAS SOLD AS A SLAVE, BUT HIS BROTHERS KEPT THE BEAUTIFUL COAT. THEY BROUGHT IT BACK TO THEIR FATHER JACOB.
LOOK, JOSEPH HAS BEEN EATEN BY WILD BEASTS!
WHAT? HIS COAT!
OH, MY SON! MY FAVORITE SON!

MEANWHILE, THE MERCHANTS TOOK JOSEPH TO EGYPT AND SOLD HIM TO POTIPHAR, THE MANAGER OF PHARAOH'S HOUSEHOLD AND CAPTAIN OF HIS GUARD.
POTIPHAR SAW SOMETHING SPECIAL IN JOSEPH. HE MADE HIM HIS HEAD SERVANT, OVERSEEING ALL HIS OFFICIAL AFFAIRS.
GOD IS WITH THAT BOY!
JOSEPH WAS SUCH A BIG HELP, POTIPHAR THEN MADE HIM HEAD OF HIS HOUSEHOLD.
GOD HAS BLESSED ME BECAUSE OF YOU, SON!
POTIPHAR'S WIFE ALSO GREW FOND OF JOSEPH. HE WAS STRONG AND HANDSOME. SO SHE TRIED TO MAKE HIM FALL IN LOVE WITH HER.
YOU'RE MY MASTER'S WIFE! I CAN'T BE WITH YOU, SO PLEASE, LEAVE ME ALONE.
SHE SCHEMED AND PLOTTED. SHE TRIED AGAIN AND AGAIN TO SEDUCE JOSEPH.
THEN ONE DAY WHEN THERE WAS NO ONE AROUND...
NO!
COME ON! I KNOW YOU LIKE ME. KISS ME!
SHE GRABBED HIM BY HIS CLOAK AND PULLED IT OFF.
LEAVE ME ALONE!!!
JOSEPH RAN OUT OF THE HOUSE IN HIS UNDERWEAR AS FAST AS HE COULD.
HELP! JOSEPH TRIED TO KISS ME!

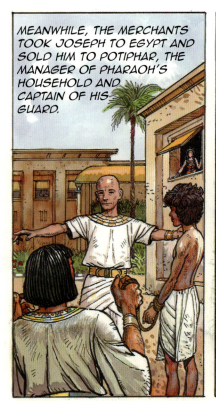

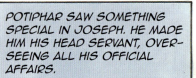

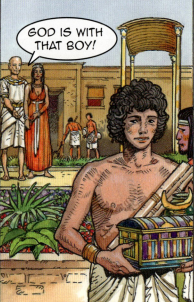

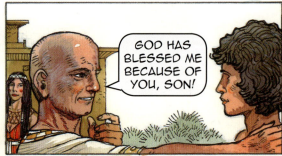

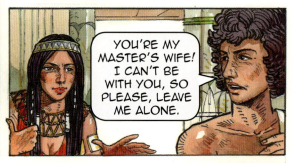

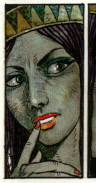

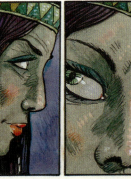

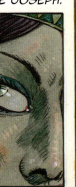

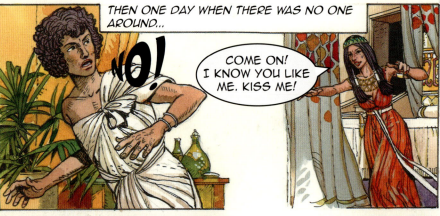

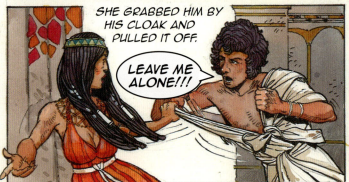

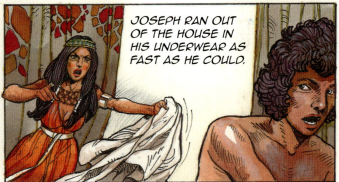

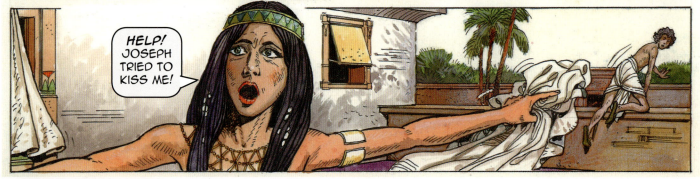

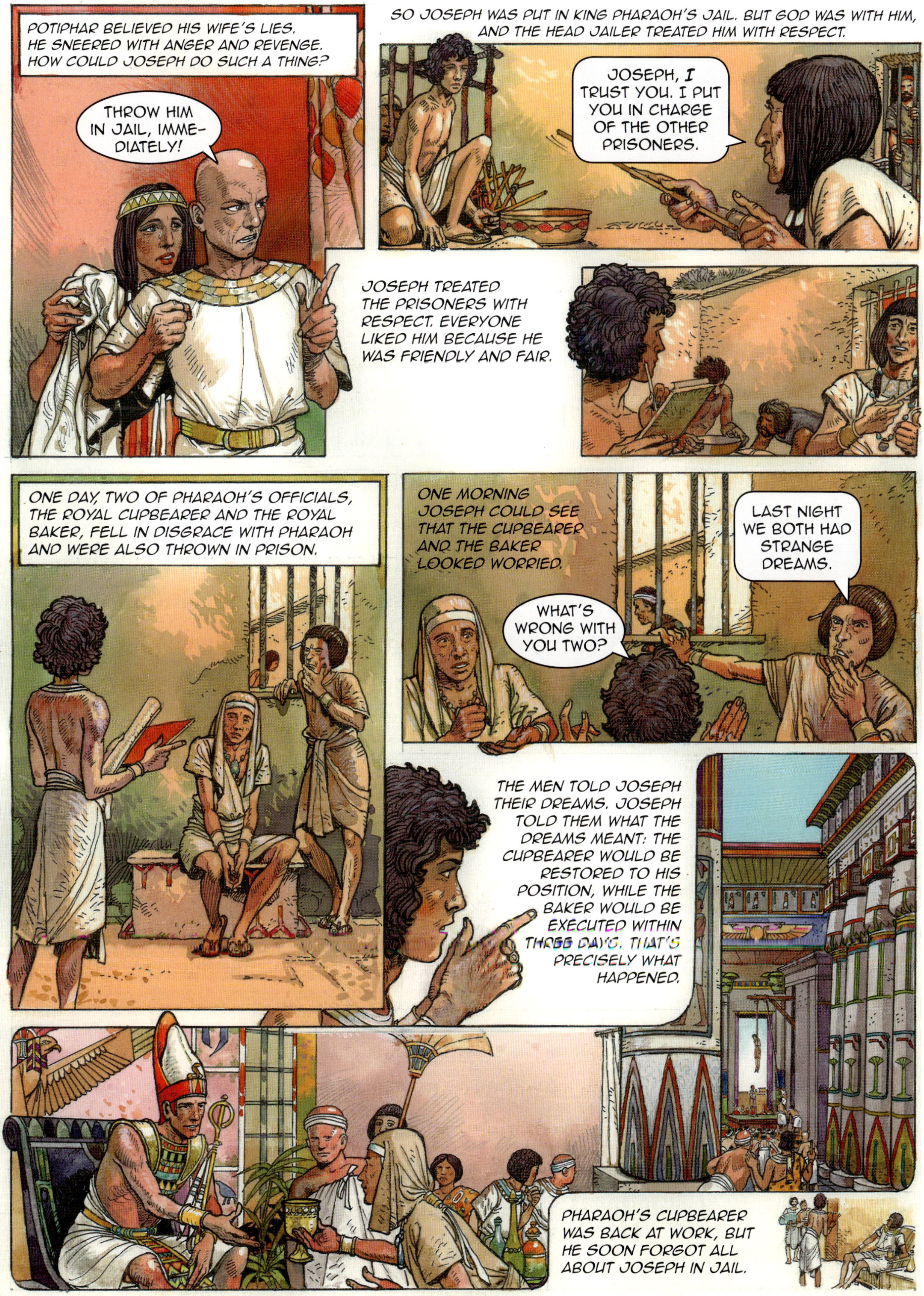
POTIPHAR BELIEVED HIS WIFE'S LIES. HE SNEERED WITH ANGER AND REVENGE. HOW COULD JOSEPH DO SUCH A THING?
THROW HIM IN JAIL, IMMEDIATELY!
SO JOSEPH WAS PUT IN KING PHARAOH'S JAIL. BUT GOD WAS WITH HIM, AND THE HEAD JAILER TREATED HIM WITH RESPECT.
JOSEPH, I TRUST YOU. I PUT YOU IN CHARGE OF THE OTHER PRISONERS.
JOSEPH TREATED THE PRISONERS WITH RESPECT. EVERYONE LIKED HIM BECAUSE HE WAS FRIENDLY AND FAIR.
ONE DAY, TWO OF PHARAOH'S OFFICIALS, THE ROYAL CUPBEARER AND THE ROYAL BAKER, FELL IN DISGRACE WITH PHARAOH AND WERE ALSO THROWN IN PRISON.
ONE MORNING JOSEPH COULD SEE THAT THE CUPBEARER AND THE BAKER LOOKED WORRIED.
LAST NIGHT WE BOTH HAD STRANGE DREAMS.
WHAT'S WRONG WITH YOU TWO?
THE MEN TOLD JOSEPH THEIR DREAMS. JOSEPH TOLD THEM WHAT THE DREAMS MEANT: THE CUPBEARER WOULD BE RESTORED TO HIS POSITION, WHILE THE BAKER WOULD BE EXECUTED WITHIN THREE DAYS. THAT'S PRECISELY WHAT HAPPENED.
PHARAOH'S CUPBEARER WAS BACK AT WORK, BUT HE SOON FORGOT ALL ABOUT JOSEPH IN JAIL.

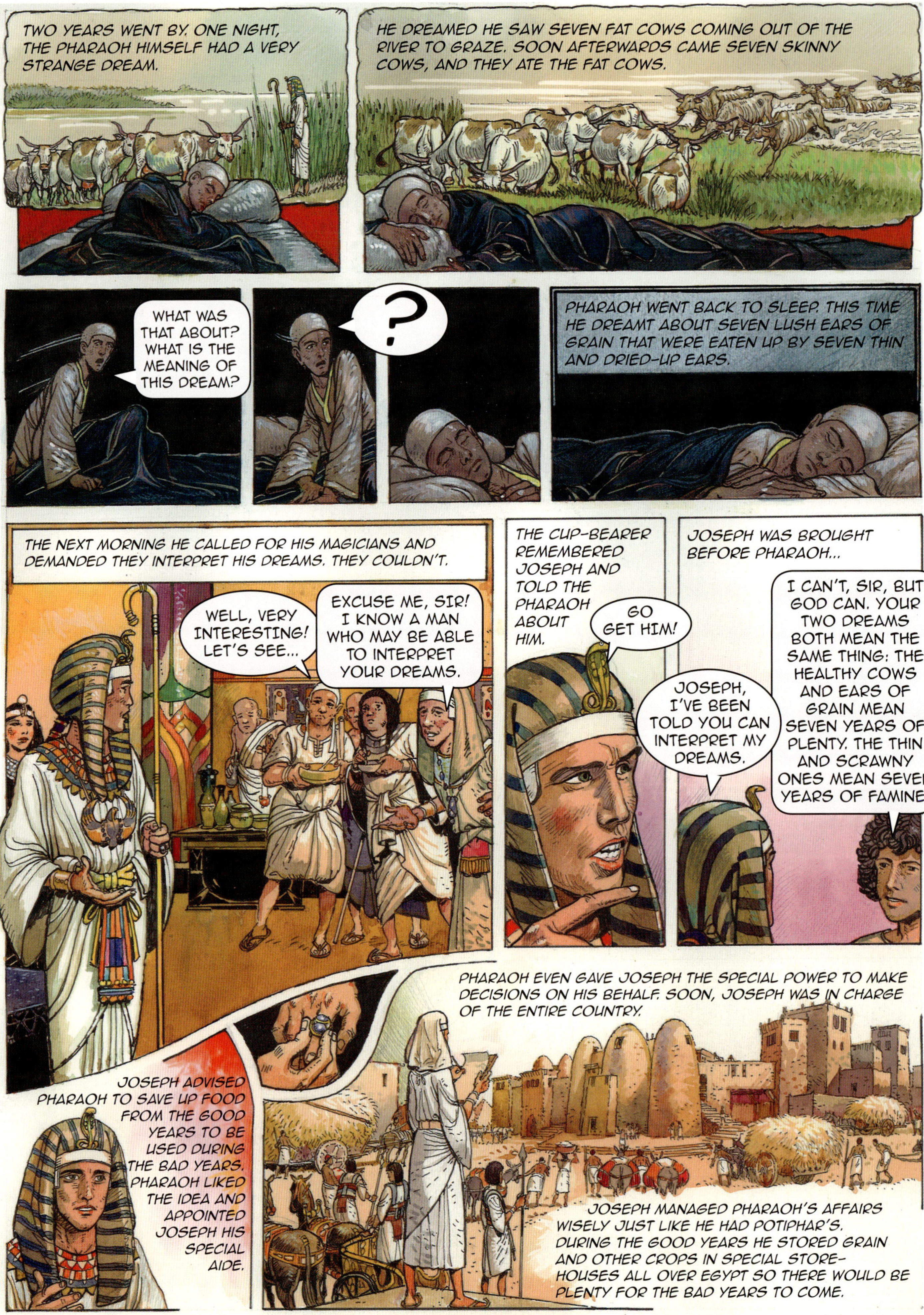
TWO YEARS WENT BY. ONE NIGHT, THE PHARAOH HIMSELF HAD A VERY STRANGE DREAM.
HE DREAMED HE SAW SEVEN FAT COWS COMING OUT OF THE RIVER TO GRAZE. SOON AFTERWARDS CAME SEVEN SKINNY COWS, AND THEY ATE THE FAT COWS.
WHAT WAS THAT ABOUT? WHAT IS THE MEANING OF THIS DREAM?
?
PHARAOH WENT BACK TO SLEEP. THIS TIME HE DREAMT ABOUT SEVEN LUSH EARS OF GRAIN THAT WERE EATEN UP BY SEVEN THIN AND DRIED-UP EARS.
THE NEXT MORNING HE CALLED FOR HIS MAGICIANS AND DEMANDED THEY INTERPRET HIS DREAMS. THEY COULDN'T.
WELL, VERY INTERESTING! LET'S SEE...
EXCUSE ME, SIR! I KNOW A MAN WHO MAY BE ABLE TO INTERPRET YOUR DREAMS.
THE CUP-BEARER REMEMBERED JOSEPH AND TOLD THE PHARAOH ABOUT HIM.
GO GET HIM!
JOSEPH WAS BROUGHT BEFORE PHARAOH...
JOSEPH, I'VE BEEN TOLD YOU CAN INTERPRET MY DREAMS.
I CAN'T, SIR, BUT GOD CAN. YOUR TWO DREAMS BOTH MEAN THE SAME THING: THE HEALTHY COWS AND EARS OF GRAIN MEAN SEVEN YEARS OF PLENTY. THE THIN AND SCRAWNY ONES MEAN SEVEN YEARS OF FAMINE.
JOSEPH ADVISED PHARAOH TO SAVE UP FOOD FROM THE GOOD YEARS TO BE USED DURING THE BAD YEARS. PHARAOH LIKED THE IDEA AND APPOINTED JOSEPH HIS SPECIAL AIDE.
PHARAOH EVEN GAVE JOSEPH THE SPECIAL POWER TO MAKE DECISIONS ON HIS BEHALF. SOON, JOSEPH WAS IN CHARGE OF THE ENTIRE COUNTRY.
JOSEPH MANAGED PHARAOH'S AFFAIRS WISELY JUST LIKE HE HAD POTIPHAR'S. DURING THE GOOD YEARS HE STORED GRAIN AND OTHER CROPS IN SPECIAL STORE-HOUSES ALL OVER EGYPT SO THERE WOULD BE PLENTY FOR THE BAD YEARS TO COME.

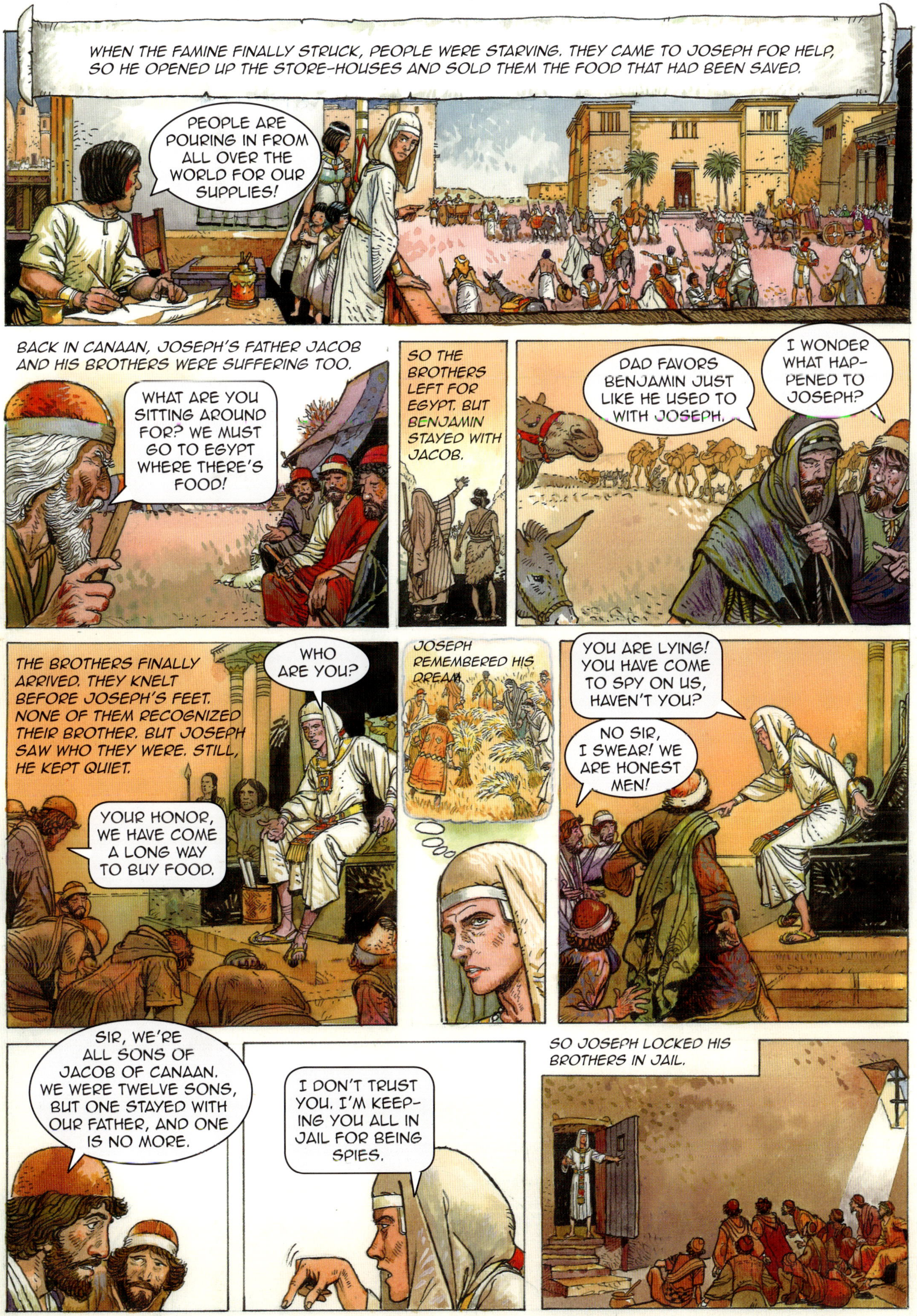
WHEN THE FAMINE FINALLY STRUCK, PEOPLE WERE STARVING. THEY CAME TO JOSEPH FOR HELP, SO HE OPENED UP THE STORE-HOUSES AND SOLD THEM THE FOOD THAT HAD BEEN SAVED.
PEOPLE ARE POURING IN FROM ALL OVER THE WORLD FOR OUR SUPPLIES!
BACK IN CANAAN, JOSEPH'S FATHER JACOB AND HIS BROTHERS WERE SUFFERING TOO.
WHAT ARE YOU SITTING AROUND FOR? WE MUST GO TO EGYPT WHERE THERE'S FOOD!
SO THE BROTHERS LEFT FOR EGYPT. BUT BENJAMIN STAYED WITH JACOB.
DAD FAVORS BENJAMIN JUST LIKE HE USED TO WITH JOSEPH.
I WONDER WHAT HAPPENED TO JOSEPH?
THE BROTHERS FINALLY ARRIVED. THEY KNELT BEFORE JOSEPH'S FEET. NONE OF THEM RECOGNIZED THEIR BROTHER. BUT JOSEPH SAW WHO THEY WERE. STILL, HE KEPT QUIET.
WHO ARE YOU?
YOUR HONOR, WE HAVE COME A LONG WAY TO BUY FOOD.
JOSEPH REMEMBERED HIS DREAM.
YOU ARE LYING! YOU HAVE COME TO SPY ON US, HAVEN'T YOU?
NO SIR, I SWEAR! WE ARE HONEST MEN!
SIR, WE'RE ALL SONS OF JACOB OF CANAAN. WE WERE TWELVE SONS, BUT ONE STAYED WITH OUR FATHER, AND ONE IS NO MORE.
I DON'T TRUST YOU. I'M KEEPING YOU ALL IN JAIL FOR BEING SPIES.
SO JOSEPH LOCKED HIS BROTHERS IN JAIL.

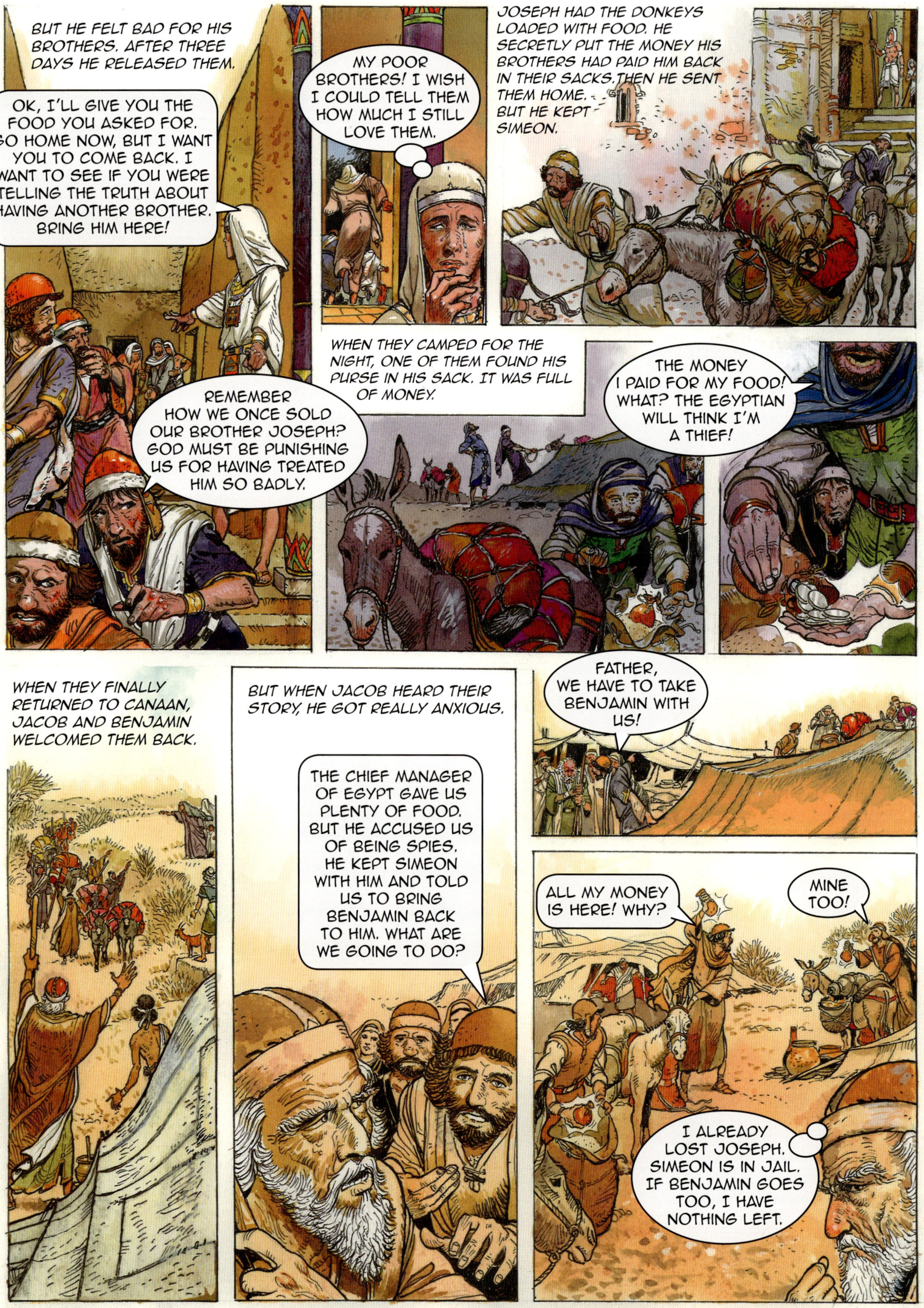
BUT HE FELT BAD FOR HIS BROTHERS. AFTER THREE DAYS HE RELEASED THEM.
OK, I'LL GIVE YOU THE FOOD YOU ASKED FOR. GO HOME NOW, BUT I WANT YOU TO COME BACK. I WANT TO SEE IF YOU WERE TELLING THE TRUTH ABOUT HAVING ANOTHER BROTHER. BRING HIM HERE!
REMEMBER HOW WE ONCE SOLD OUR BROTHER JOSEPH? GOD MUST BE PUNISHING US FOR HAVING TREATED HIM SO BADLY.
MY POOR BROTHERS! I WISH I COULD TELL THEM HOW MUCH I STILL LOVE THEM.
JOSEPH HAD THE DONKEYS LOADED WITH FOOD. HE SECRETLY PUT THE MONEY HIS BROTHERS HAD PAID HIM BACK IN THEIR SACKS. THEN HE SENT THEM HOME. BUT HE KEPT SIMEON.
WHEN THEY CAMPED FOR THE NIGHT, ONE OF THEM FOUND HIS PURSE IN HIS SACK. IT WAS FULL OF MONEY.
THE MONEY I PAID FOR MY FOOD! WHAT? THE EGYPTIAN WILL THINK I'M A THIEF!
WHEN THEY FINALLY RETURNED TO CANAAN, JACOB AND BENJAMIN WELCOMED THEM BACK.
BUT WHEN JACOB HEARD THEIR STORY, HE GOT REALLY ANXIOUS.
THE CHIEF MANAGER OF EGYPT GAVE US PLENTY OF FOOD. BUT HE ACCUSED US OF BEING SPIES. HE KEPT SIMEON WITH HIM AND TOLD US TO BRING BENJAMIN BACK TO HIM. WHAT ARE WE GOING TO DO?
FATHER, WE HAVE TO TAKE BENJAMIN WITH US!
ALL MY MONEY IS HERE! WHY?
MINE TOO!
I ALREADY LOST JOSEPH. SIMEON IS IN JAIL. IF BENJAMIN GOES TOO, I HAVE NOTHING LEFT.

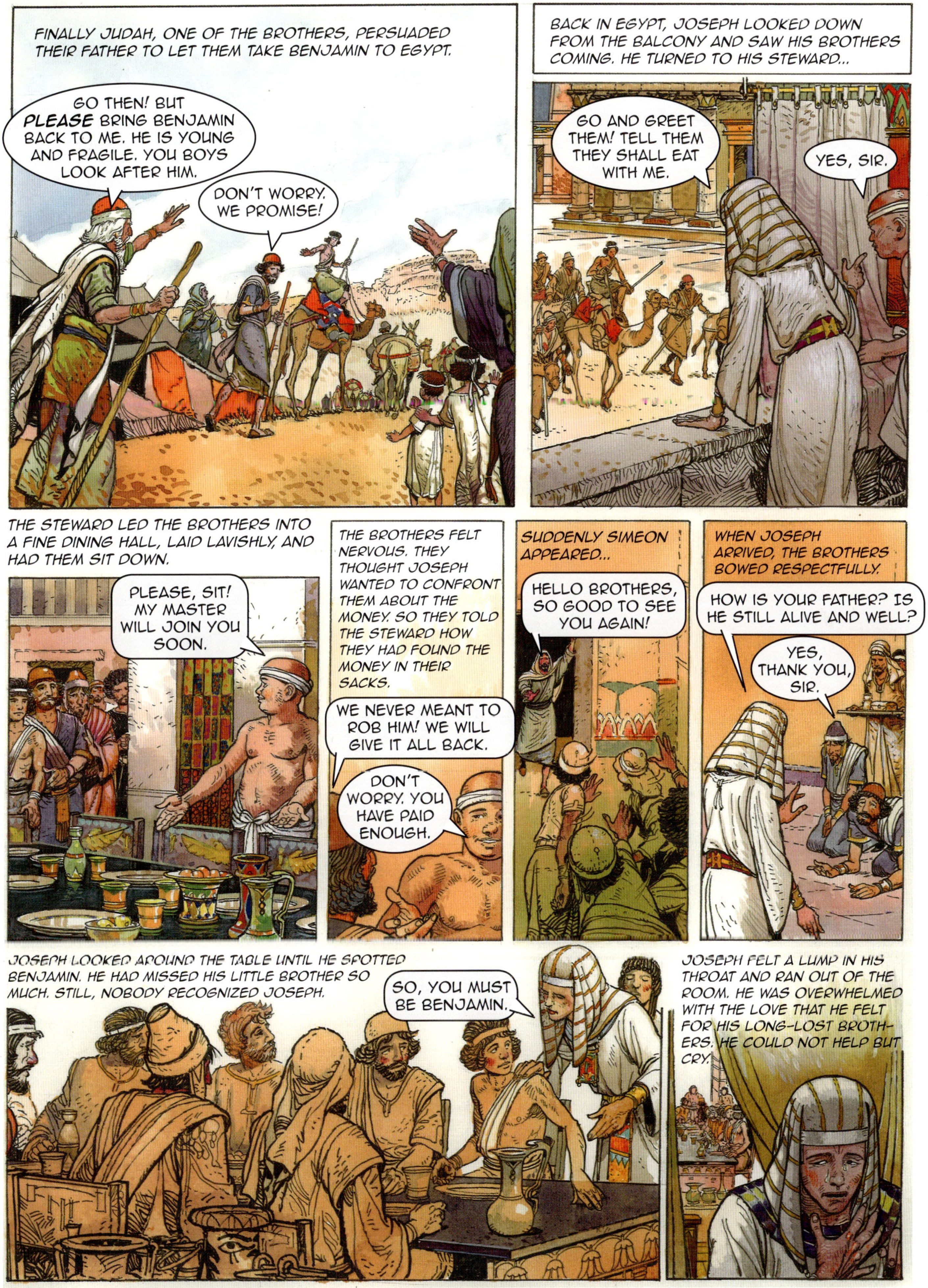
FINALLY JUDAH, ONE OF THE BROTHERS, PERSUADED THEIR FATHER TO LET THEM TAKE BENJAMIN TO EGYPT.
GO THEN! BUT **PLEASE** BRING BENJAMIN BACK TO ME. HE IS YOUNG AND FRAGILE. YOU BOYS LOOK AFTER HIM.
DON'T WORRY. WE PROMISE!
BACK IN EGYPT, JOSEPH LOOKED DOWN FROM THE BALCONY AND SAW HIS BROTHERS COMING. HE TURNED TO HIS STEWARD...
GO AND GREET THEM! TELL THEM THEY SHALL EAT WITH ME.
YES, SIR.
THE STEWARD LED THE BROTHERS INTO A FINE DINING HALL, LAID LAVISHLY, AND HAD THEM SIT DOWN.
PLEASE, SIT! MY MASTER WILL JOIN YOU SOON.
THE BROTHERS FELT NERVOUS. THEY THOUGHT JOSEPH WANTED TO CONFRONT THEM ABOUT THE MONEY. SO THEY TOLD THE STEWARD HOW THEY HAD FOUND THE MONEY IN THEIR SACKS.
WE NEVER MEANT TO ROB HIM! WE WILL GIVE IT ALL BACK.
DON'T WORRY. YOU HAVE PAID ENOUGH.
SUDDENLY SIMEON APPEARED...
HELLO BROTHERS, SO GOOD TO SEE YOU AGAIN!
WHEN JOSEPH ARRIVED, THE BROTHERS BOWED RESPECTFULLY.
HOW IS YOUR FATHER? IS HE STILL ALIVE AND WELL?
YES, THANK YOU, SIR.
JOSEPH LOOKED AROUND THE TABLE UNTIL HE SPOTTED BENJAMIN. HE HAD MISSED HIS LITTLE BROTHER SO MUCH. STILL, NOBODY RECOGNIZED JOSEPH.
SO, YOU MUST BE BENJAMIN.
JOSEPH FELT A LUMP IN HIS THROAT AND RAN OUT OF THE ROOM. HE WAS OVERWHELMED WITH THE LOVE THAT HE FELT FOR HIS LONG-LOST BROTHERS. HE COULD NOT HELP BUT CRY.

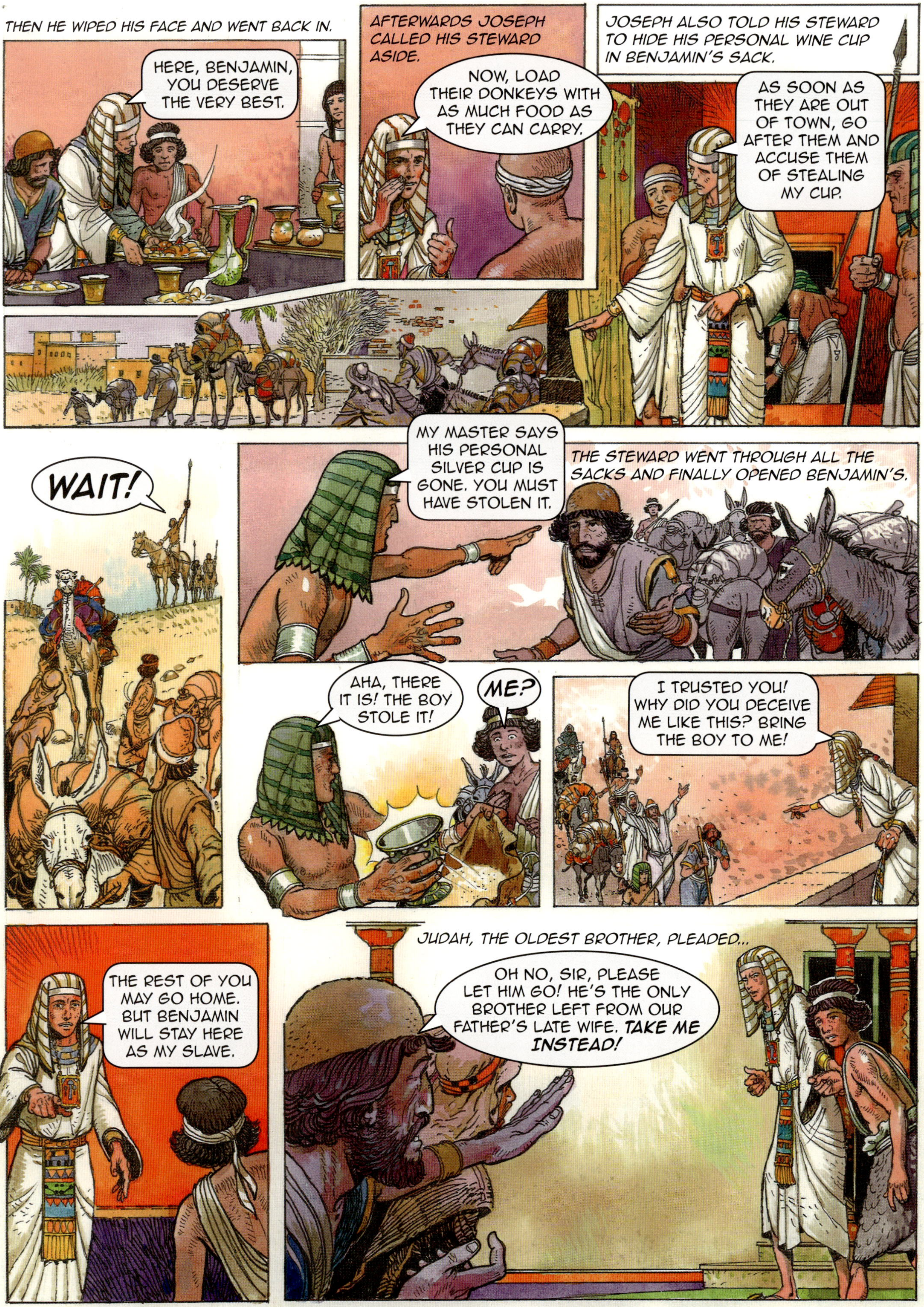
THEN HE WIPED HIS FACE AND WENT BACK IN.
HERE, BENJAMIN, YOU DESERVE THE VERY BEST.
AFTERWARDS JOSEPH CALLED HIS STEWARD ASIDE.
NOW, LOAD THEIR DONKEYS WITH AS MUCH FOOD AS THEY CAN CARRY.
JOSEPH ALSO TOLD HIS STEWARD TO HIDE HIS PERSONAL WINE CUP IN BENJAMIN'S SACK.
AS SOON AS THEY ARE OUT OF TOWN, GO AFTER THEM AND ACCUSE THEM OF STEALING MY CUP.
WAIT!
MY MASTER SAYS HIS PERSONAL SILVER CUP IS GONE. YOU MUST HAVE STOLEN IT.
THE STEWARD WENT THROUGH ALL THE SACKS AND FINALLY OPENED BENJAMIN'S.
AHA, THERE IT IS! THE BOY STOLE IT!
ME?
I TRUSTED YOU! WHY DID YOU DECEIVE ME LIKE THIS? BRING THE BOY TO ME!
THE REST OF YOU MAY GO HOME. BUT BENJAMIN WILL STAY HERE AS MY SLAVE.
JUDAH, THE OLDEST BROTHER, PLEADED...
OH NO, SIR, PLEASE LET HIM GO! HE'S THE ONLY BROTHER LEFT FROM OUR FATHER'S LATE WIFE. TAKE ME INSTEAD!

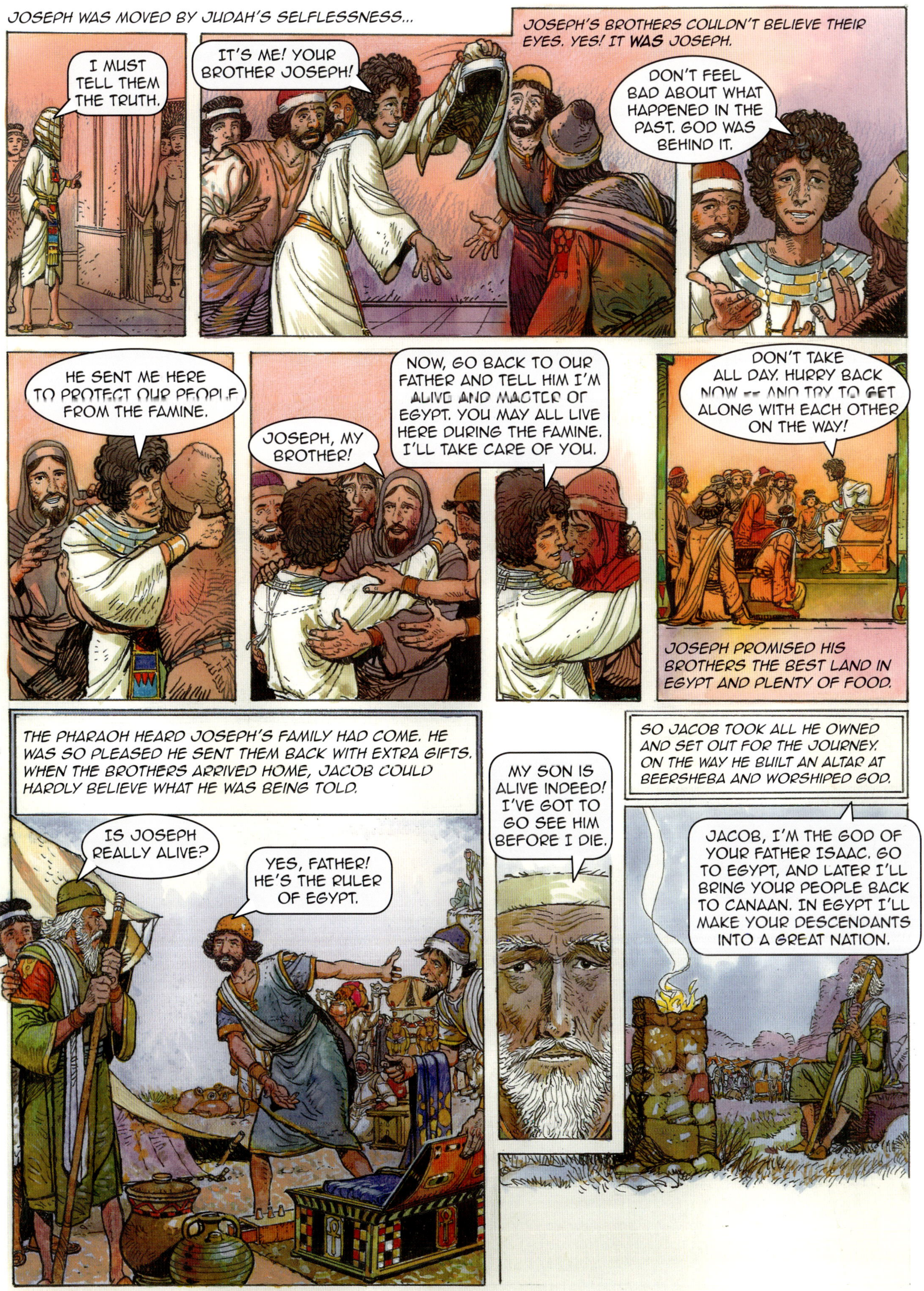
JOSEPH WAS MOVED BY JUDAH'S SELFLESSNESS...
I MUST TELL THEM THE TRUTH.
IT'S ME! YOUR BROTHER JOSEPH!
JOSEPH'S BROTHERS COULDN'T BELIEVE THEIR EYES. YES! IT WAS JOSEPH.
DON'T FEEL BAD ABOUT WHAT HAPPENED IN THE PAST. GOD WAS BEHIND IT.
HE SENT ME HERE TO PROTECT OUR PEOPLE FROM THE FAMINE.
JOSEPH, MY BROTHER!
NOW, GO BACK TO OUR FATHER AND TELL HIM I'M ALIVE AND MASTER OF EGYPT. YOU MAY ALL LIVE HERE DURING THE FAMINE. I'LL TAKE CARE OF YOU.
DON'T TAKE ALL DAY. HURRY BACK NOW -- AND TRY TO GET ALONG WITH EACH OTHER ON THE WAY!
JOSEPH PROMISED HIS BROTHERS THE BEST LAND IN EGYPT AND PLENTY OF FOOD.
THE PHARAOH HEARD JOSEPH'S FAMILY HAD COME. HE WAS SO PLEASED HE SENT THEM BACK WITH EXTRA GIFTS. WHEN THE BROTHERS ARRIVED HOME, JACOB COULD HARDLY BELIEVE WHAT HE WAS BEING TOLD.
IS JOSEPH REALLY ALIVE?
YES, FATHER! HE'S THE RULER OF EGYPT.
MY SON IS ALIVE INDEED! I'VE GOT TO GO SEE HIM BEFORE I DIE.
SO JACOB TOOK ALL HE OWNED AND SET OUT FOR THE JOURNEY. ON THE WAY HE BUILT AN ALTAR AT BEERSHEBA AND WORSHIPED GOD.
JACOB, I'M THE GOD OF YOUR FATHER ISAAC. GO TO EGYPT, AND LATER I'LL BRING YOUR PEOPLE BACK TO CANAAN. IN EGYPT I'LL MAKE YOUR DESCENDANTS INTO A GREAT NATION.

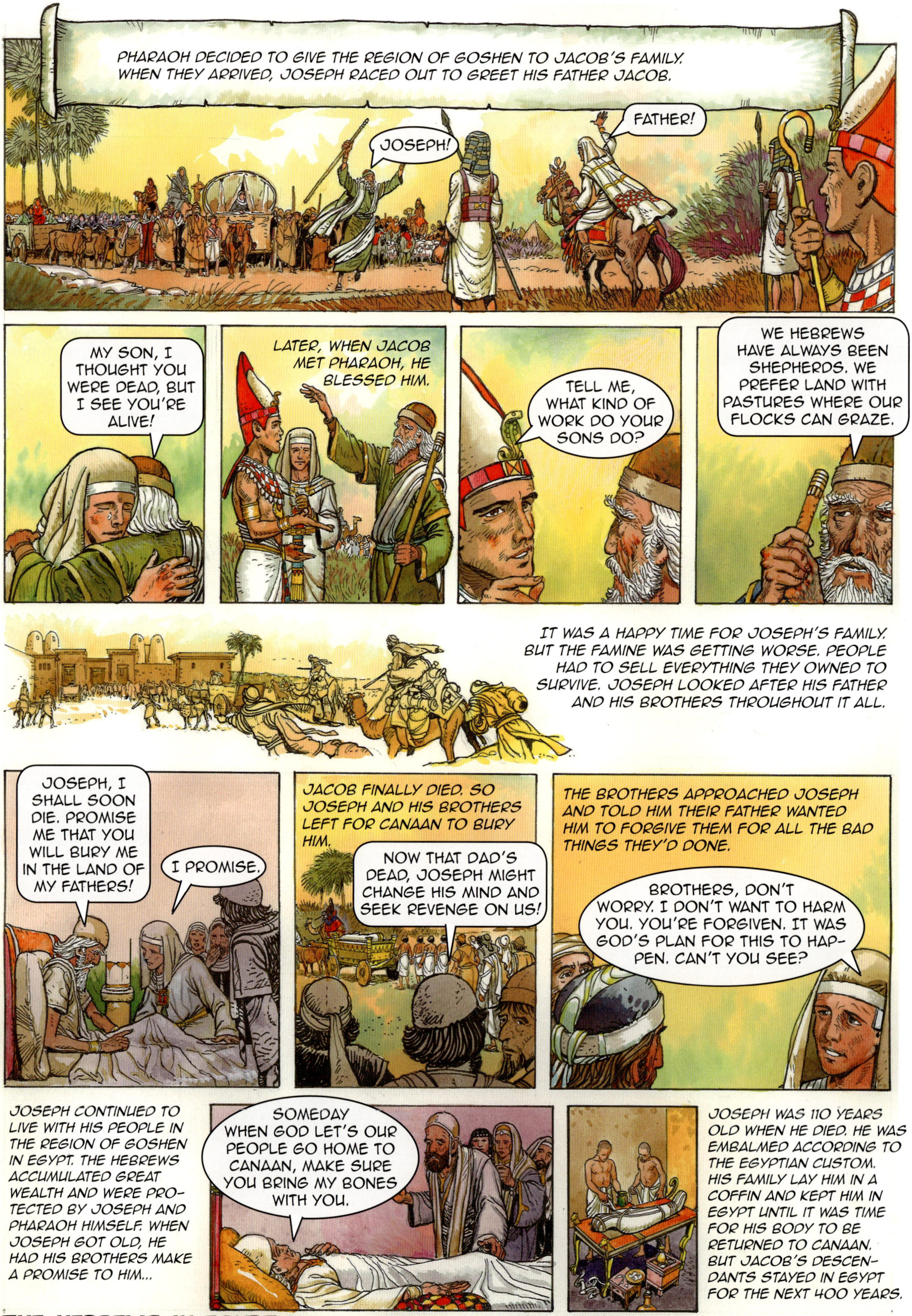
PHARAOH DECIDED TO GIVE THE REGION OF GOSHEN TO JACOB'S FAMILY. WHEN THEY ARRIVED, JOSEPH RACED OUT TO GREET HIS FATHER JACOB.
JOSEPH!
FATHER!
MY SON, I THOUGHT YOU WERE DEAD, BUT I SEE YOU'RE ALIVE!
LATER, WHEN JACOB MET PHARAOH, HE BLESSED HIM.
TELL ME, WHAT KIND OF WORK DO YOUR SONS DO?
WE HEBREWS HAVE ALWAYS BEEN SHEPHERDS. WE PREFER LAND WITH PASTURES WHERE OUR FLOCKS CAN GRAZE.
IT WAS A HAPPY TIME FOR JOSEPH'S FAMILY. BUT THE FAMINE WAS GETTING WORSE. PEOPLE HAD TO SELL EVERYTHING THEY OWNED TO SURVIVE. JOSEPH LOOKED AFTER HIS FATHER AND HIS BROTHERS THROUGHOUT IT ALL.
JOSEPH, I SHALL SOON DIE. PROMISE ME THAT YOU WILL BURY ME IN THE LAND OF MY FATHERS!
I PROMISE.
JACOB FINALLY DIED. SO JOSEPH AND HIS BROTHERS LEFT FOR CANAAN TO BURY HIM.
NOW THAT DAD'S DEAD, JOSEPH MIGHT CHANGE HIS MIND AND SEEK REVENGE ON US!
THE BROTHERS APPROACHED JOSEPH AND TOLD HIM THEIR FATHER WANTED HIM TO FORGIVE THEM FOR ALL THE BAD THINGS THEY'D DONE.
BROTHERS, DON'T WORRY. I DON'T WANT TO HARM YOU. YOU'RE FORGIVEN. IT WAS GOD'S PLAN FOR THIS TO HAPPEN. CAN'T YOU SEE?
JOSEPH CONTINUED TO LIVE WITH HIS PEOPLE IN THE REGION OF GOSHEN IN EGYPT. THE HEBREWS ACCUMULATED GREAT WEALTH AND WERE PROTECTED BY JOSEPH AND PHARAOH HIMSELF. WHEN JOSEPH GOT OLD, HE HAD HIS BROTHERS MAKE A PROMISE TO HIM...
SOMEDAY WHEN GOD LET'S OUR PEOPLE GO HOME TO CANAAN, MAKE SURE YOU BRING MY BONES WITH YOU.
JOSEPH WAS 110 YEARS OLD WHEN HE DIED. HE WAS EMBALMED ACCORDING TO THE EGYPTIAN CUSTOM. HIS FAMILY LAY HIM IN A COFFIN AND KEPT HIM IN EGYPT UNTIL IT WAS TIME FOR HIS BODY TO BE RETURNED TO CANAAN. BUT JACOB'S DESCENDANTS STAYED IN EGYPT FOR THE NEXT 400 YEARS.

AFTER JOSEPH DIED, EGYPT CHANGED A GREAT DEAL. THE DESCENDANTS OF JOSEPH'S FAMILY GREW AND GREW. SOON, THERE WAS A LARGE POPULATION OF HEBREWS LIVING IN EGYPT. THE NEW PHARAOH DID NOT LIKE THIS.
IF OUR ENEMIES ATTACK US, THEY MIGHT ABANDON US, OR WORSE, JOIN THEM!
WHY DON'T WE TURN THEM INTO SLAVES? THAT WAY THEY WILL HAVE TO DO WHAT WE SAY. THAT'S THE SOLUTION!
AND SO, THE HEBREWS BECAME SLAVES...
HEY YOU! MOVE! FASTER!
ARRRRGH!
THEN PHARAOH WENT A STEP FURTHER. HE CALLED IN TWO MIDWIVES...
FROM NOW ON YOU MUST KILL EVERY NEWBORN BOY AMONG THE HEBREWS.
THE MIDWIVES WERE GOD-FEARING WOMEN. THEY DIDN'T DO WHAT PHARAOH HAD TOLD THEM.
ANOTHER BEAUTIFUL BOY! MAY GOD BLESS YOU!
PHARAOH CALLED THE MIDWIVES IN.
DIDN'T I TELL YOU TO KILL EVERY NEWBORN BOY? HOW COME YOU DIDN'T OBEY MY ORDERS?
SIR, THE HEBREW WOMEN ARE TOO QUICK. THEIR BABIES ARE BORN BEFORE WE EVER ARRIVE. IT'S NO USE!
NEARBY, A HEBREW FAMILY HEARD ABOUT PHARAOH'S ORDERS. THEY'D JUST HAD A SON, SO THE MOTHER HID HIM FOR SEVERAL MONTHS.
SHE PRAYED THE PHARAOH WOULD NOT FIND HIM AND KILL HIM.

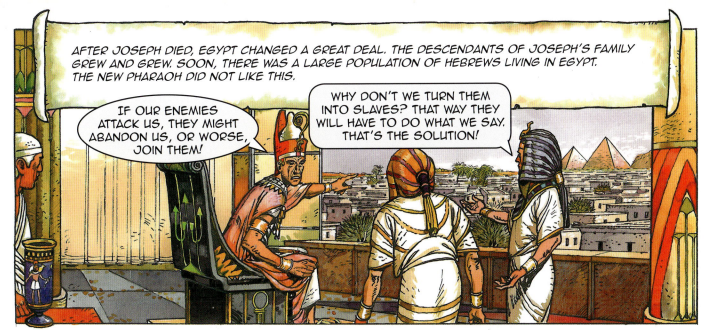

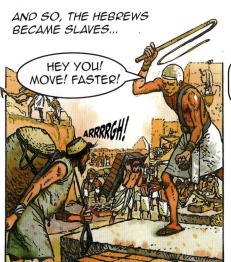

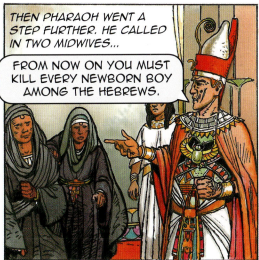

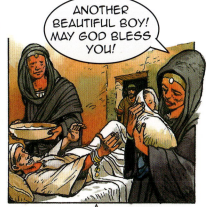

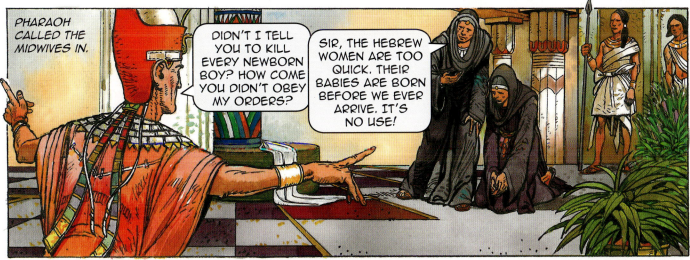

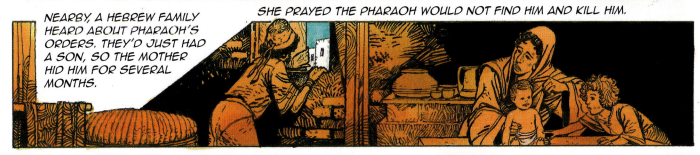

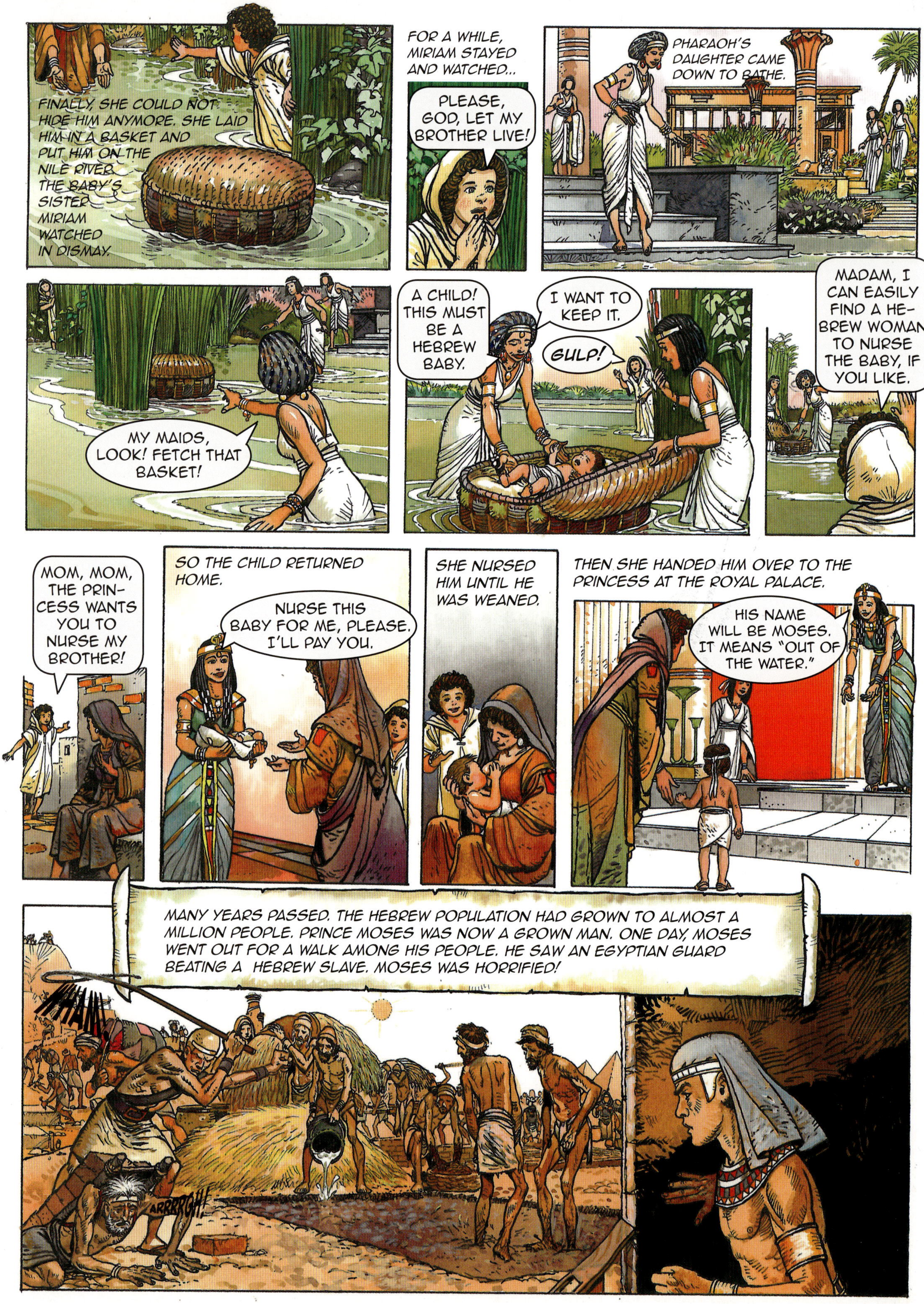
FINALLY, SHE COULD NOT HIDE HIM ANYMORE. SHE LAID HIM IN A BASKET AND PUT HIM ON THE NILE RIVER. THE BABY'S SISTER MIRIAM WATCHED IN DISMAY.
FOR A WHILE, MIRIAM STAYED AND WATCHED...
PLEASE, GOD, LET MY BROTHER LIVE!
PHARAOH'S DAUGHTER CAME DOWN TO BATHE.
MY MAIDS, LOOK! FETCH THAT BASKET!
A CHILD! THIS MUST BE A HEBREW BABY.
I WANT TO KEEP IT.
GULP!
MADAM, I CAN EASILY FIND A HEBREW WOMAN TO NURSE THE BABY, IF YOU LIKE.
MOM, MOM, THE PRINCESS WANTS YOU TO NURSE MY BROTHER!
SO THE CHILD RETURNED HOME.
NURSE THIS BABY FOR ME, PLEASE. I'LL PAY YOU.
SHE NURSED HIM UNTIL HE WAS WEANED.
THEN SHE HANDED HIM OVER TO THE PRINCESS AT THE ROYAL PALACE.
HIS NAME WILL BE MOSES. IT MEANS "OUT OF THE WATER."
MANY YEARS PASSED. THE HEBREW POPULATION HAD GROWN TO ALMOST A MILLION PEOPLE. PRINCE MOSES WAS NOW A GROWN MAN. ONE DAY, MOSES WENT OUT FOR A WALK AMONG HIS PEOPLE. HE SAW AN EGYPTIAN GUARD BEATING A HEBREW SLAVE. MOSES WAS HORRIFIED!
WHAM!
ARRRRGH!

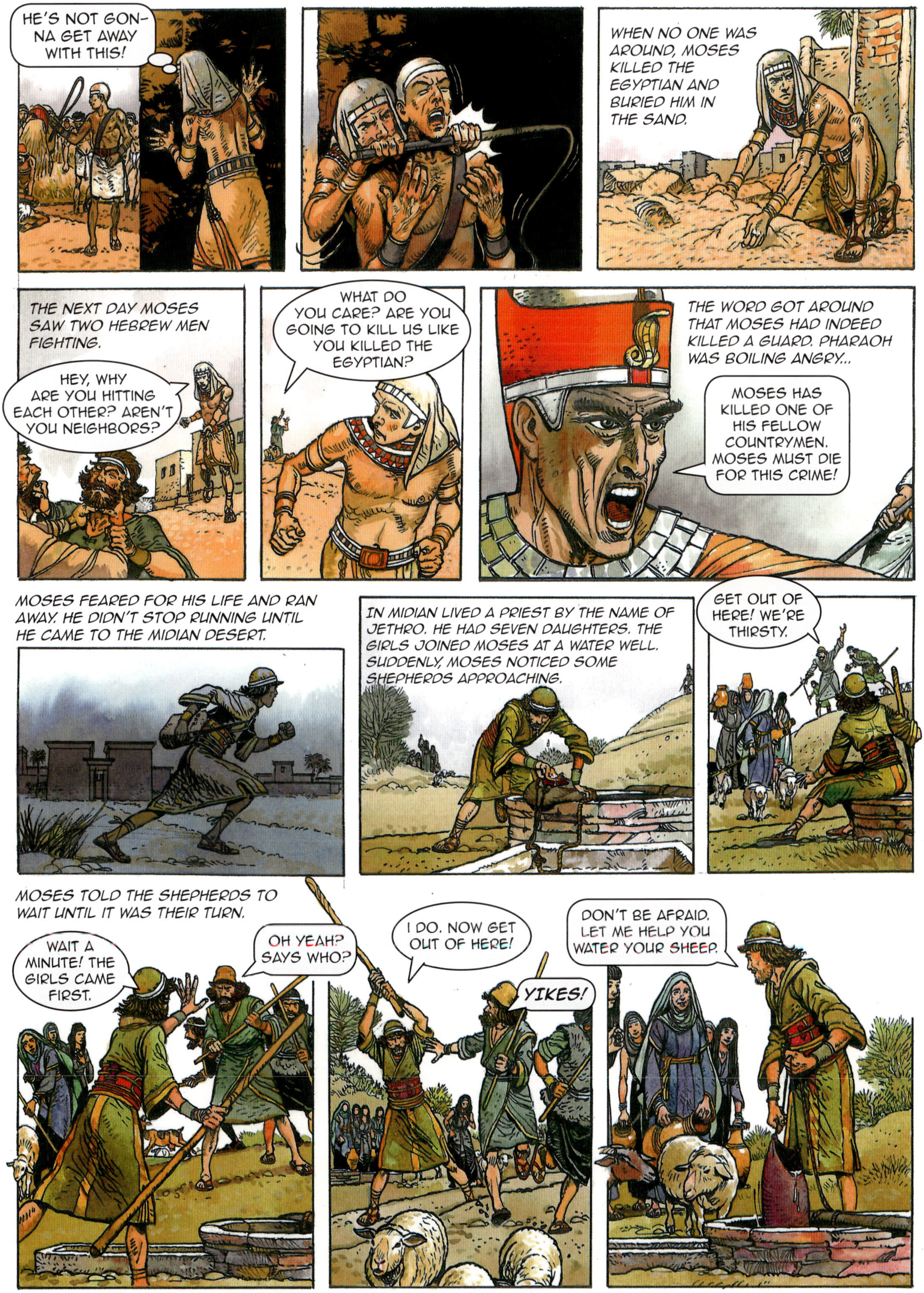
HE'S NOT GON-NA GET AWAY WITH THIS!
WHEN NO ONE WAS AROUND, MOSES KILLED THE EGYPTIAN AND BURIED HIM IN THE SAND.
THE NEXT DAY MOSES SAW TWO HEBREW MEN FIGHTING.
HEY, WHY ARE YOU HITTING EACH OTHER? AREN'T YOU NEIGHBORS?
WHAT DO YOU CARE? ARE YOU GOING TO KILL US LIKE YOU KILLED THE EGYPTIAN?
THE WORD GOT AROUND THAT MOSES HAD INDEED KILLED A GUARD. PHARAOH WAS BOILING ANGRY...
MOSES HAS KILLED ONE OF HIS FELLOW COUNTRYMEN. MOSES MUST DIE FOR THIS CRIME!
MOSES FEARED FOR HIS LIFE AND RAN AWAY. HE DIDN'T STOP RUNNING UNTIL HE CAME TO THE MIDIAN DESERT.
IN MIDIAN LIVED A PRIEST BY THE NAME OF JETHRO. HE HAD SEVEN DAUGHTERS. THE GIRLS JOINED MOSES AT A WATER WELL. SUDDENLY, MOSES NOTICED SOME SHEPHERDS APPROACHING.
GET OUT OF HERE! WE'RE THIRSTY.
MOSES TOLD THE SHEPHERDS TO WAIT UNTIL IT WAS THEIR TURN.
WAIT A MINUTE! THE GIRLS CAME FIRST.
OH YEAH? SAYS WHO?
I DO. NOW GET OUT OF HERE!
YIKES!
DON'T BE AFRAID. LET ME HELP YOU WATER YOUR SHEEP.

THE GIRLS INVITED MOSES TO THEIR FATHER'S HOUSE.
THAT DIDN'T TAKE LONG.
A MAN HELPED US WATER THE SHEEP.
JETHRO WAS THANKFUL AND LET MOSES STAY FOR DINNER. HE TOLD HIM TO STAY AS LONG AS HE LIKED.
EAT UP, MOSES!
I'LL EVEN GIVE YOU MY DAUGHTER ZIPPORAH FOR A WIFE.
SO MOSES MARRIED ZIPPORAH AND TOGETHER THEY HAD A SON.
BACK IN EGYPT, A NEW PHARAOH TOOK OVER. BUT STILL, THE HEBREWS WERE SUFFERING AS SLAVES. THEY WERE TREATED WORSE THAN EVER BEFORE. GOD WAS SADDENED BY THIS. SO, HE DECIDED TO DO SOMETHING ABOUT IT.
ONE DAY MOSES WAS OUT IN THE DESERT WITH HIS FLOCK. HE SAW A FLASH AND LOOKED UP.
SOMETHING'S ON FIRE! I'LL GO AND CHECK IT OUT.
A BURNING BUSH! BUT WHY ISN'T IT BEING CON-SUMED?
MOSES! MOSES!
I'M RIGHT HERE.
DO NOT COME ANY CLOSER. TAKE OFF YOUR SANDALS. YOU'RE ON HOLY GROUND.
I'M THE GOD OF YOUR FATHERS -- THE GOD OF ABRAHAM, ISAAC, AND JACOB. LISTEN TO ME!
I HAVE SEEN HOW MY PEOPLE SUFFER IN EGYPT. I KNOW THEIR PAIN.
MOSES HID HIS FACE. HE WAS AFRAID TO LOOK AT GOD.

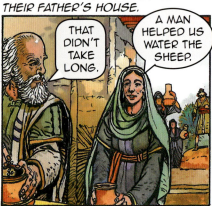

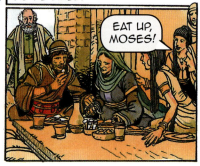

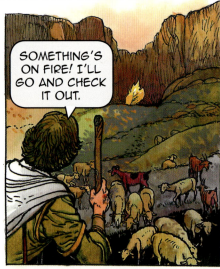

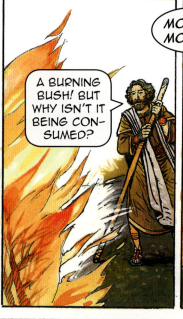

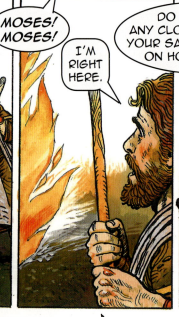

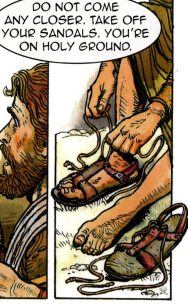

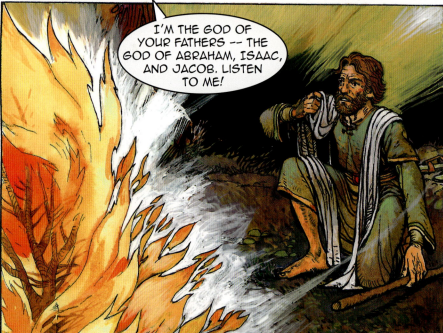

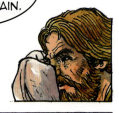

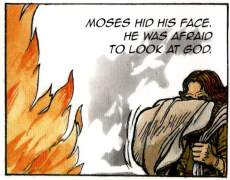

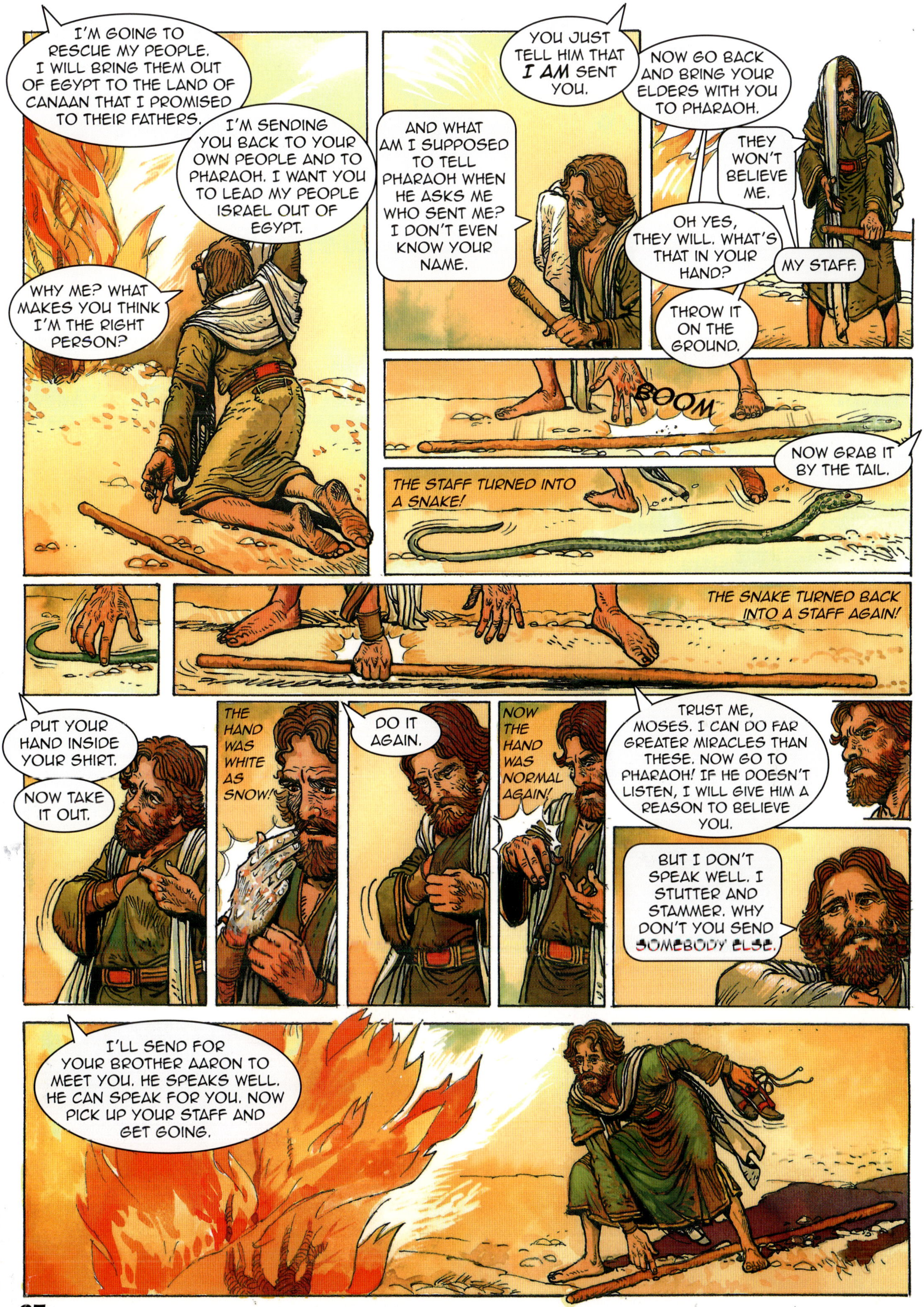

I'M GOING TO RESCUE MY PEOPLE. I WILL BRING THEM OUT OF EGYPT TO THE LAND OF CANAAN THAT I PROMISED TO THEIR FATHERS.
I'M SENDING YOU BACK TO YOUR OWN PEOPLE AND TO PHARAOH. I WANT YOU TO LEAD MY PEOPLE ISRAEL OUT OF EGYPT.
WHY ME? WHAT MAKES YOU THINK I'M THE RIGHT PERSON?
AND WHAT AM I SUPPOSED TO TELL PHARAOH WHEN HE ASKS ME WHO SENT ME? I DON'T EVEN KNOW YOUR NAME.
YOU JUST TELL HIM THAT **I AM** SENT YOU.
NOW GO BACK AND BRING YOUR ELDERS WITH YOU TO PHARAOH.
THEY WON'T BELIEVE ME.
OH YES, THEY WILL. WHAT'S THAT IN YOUR HAND?
MY STAFF.
THROW IT ON THE GROUND.
BOOM
THE STAFF TURNED INTO A SNAKE!
NOW GRAB IT BY THE TAIL.
THE SNAKE TURNED BACK INTO A STAFF AGAIN!
PUT YOUR HAND INSIDE YOUR SHIRT.
NOW TAKE IT OUT.
THE HAND WAS WHITE AS SNOW!
DO IT AGAIN.
NOW THE HAND WAS NORMAL AGAIN!
TRUST ME, MOSES. I CAN DO FAR GREATER MIRACLES THAN THESE. NOW GO TO PHARAOH! IF HE DOESN'T LISTEN, I WILL GIVE HIM A REASON TO BELIEVE YOU.
BUT I DON'T SPEAK WELL. I STUTTER AND STAMMER. WHY DON'T YOU SEND SOMEBODY ELSE.
I'LL SEND FOR YOUR BROTHER AARON TO MEET YOU. HE SPEAKS WELL. HE CAN SPEAK FOR YOU. NOW PICK UP YOUR STAFF AND GET GOING.

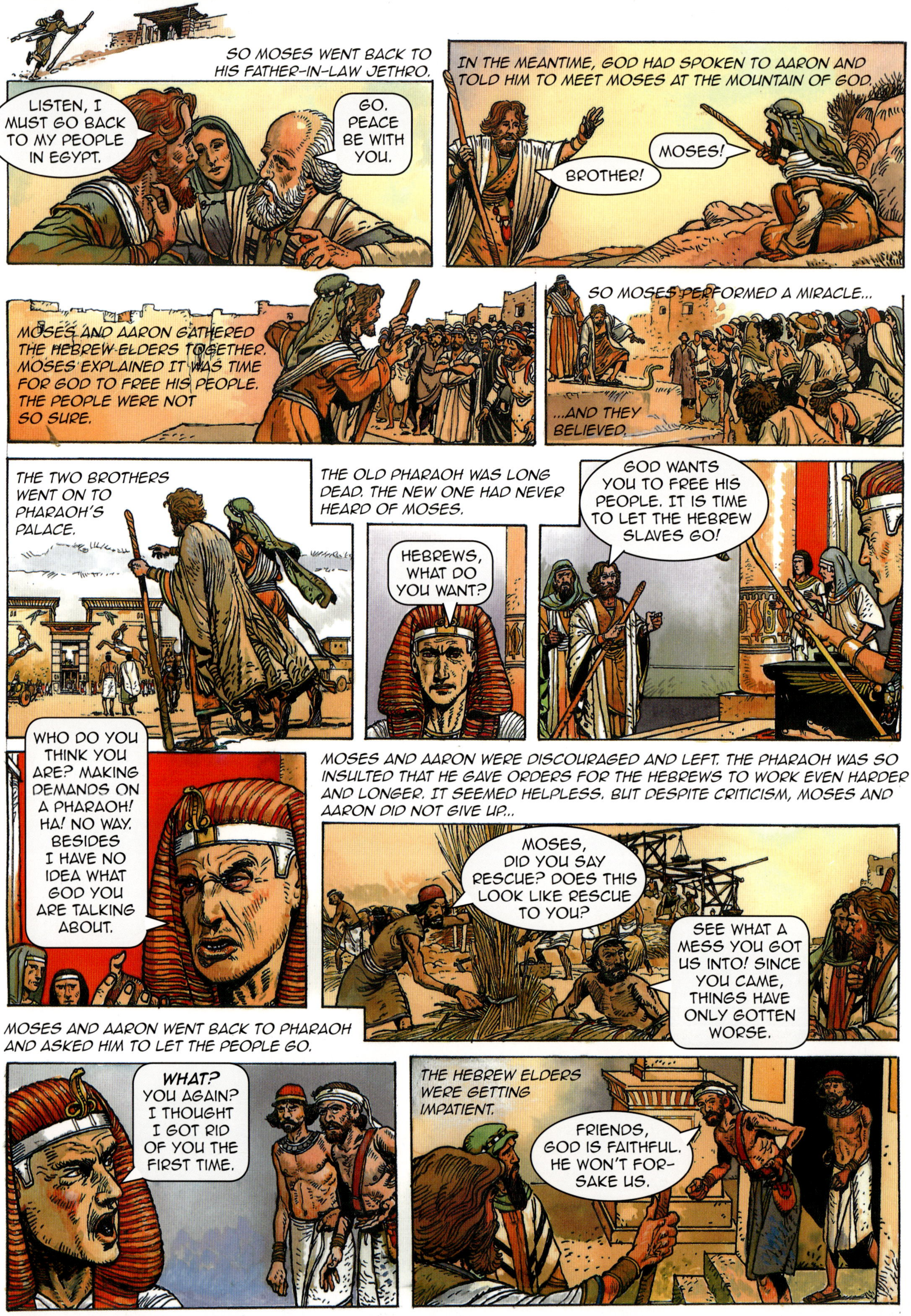
SO MOSES WENT BACK TO HIS FATHER-IN-LAW JETHRO.
LISTEN, I MUST GO BACK TO MY PEOPLE IN EGYPT.
GO. PEACE BE WITH YOU.
IN THE MEANTIME, GOD HAD SPOKEN TO AARON AND TOLD HIM TO MEET MOSES AT THE MOUNTAIN OF GOD.
MOSES!
BROTHER!
MOSES AND AARON GATHERED THE HEBREW ELDERS TOGETHER. MOSES EXPLAINED IT WAS TIME FOR GOD TO FREE HIS PEOPLE. THE PEOPLE WERE NOT SO SURE.
SO MOSES PERFORMED A MIRACLE...
...AND THEY BELIEVED.
THE TWO BROTHERS WENT ON TO PHARAOH'S PALACE.
THE OLD PHARAOH WAS LONG DEAD. THE NEW ONE HAD NEVER HEARD OF MOSES.
HEBREWS, WHAT DO YOU WANT?
GOD WANTS YOU TO FREE HIS PEOPLE. IT IS TIME TO LET THE HEBREW SLAVES GO!
WHO DO YOU THINK YOU ARE? MAKING DEMANDS ON A PHARAOH! HA! NO WAY. BESIDES I HAVE NO IDEA WHAT GOD YOU ARE TALKING ABOUT.
MOSES AND AARON WERE DISCOURAGED AND LEFT. THE PHARAOH WAS SO INSULTED THAT HE GAVE ORDERS FOR THE HEBREWS TO WORK EVEN HARDER AND LONGER. IT SEEMED HELPLESS. BUT DESPITE CRITICISM, MOSES AND AARON DID NOT GIVE UP...
MOSES, DID YOU SAY RESCUE? DOES THIS LOOK LIKE RESCUE TO YOU?
SEE WHAT A MESS YOU GOT US INTO! SINCE YOU CAME, THINGS HAVE ONLY GOTTEN WORSE.
MOSES AND AARON WENT BACK TO PHARAOH AND ASKED HIM TO LET THE PEOPLE GO.
WHAT? YOU AGAIN? I THOUGHT I GOT RID OF YOU THE FIRST TIME.
THE HEBREW ELDERS WERE GETTING IMPATIENT.
FRIENDS, GOD IS FAITHFUL. HE WON'T FOR-SAKE US.

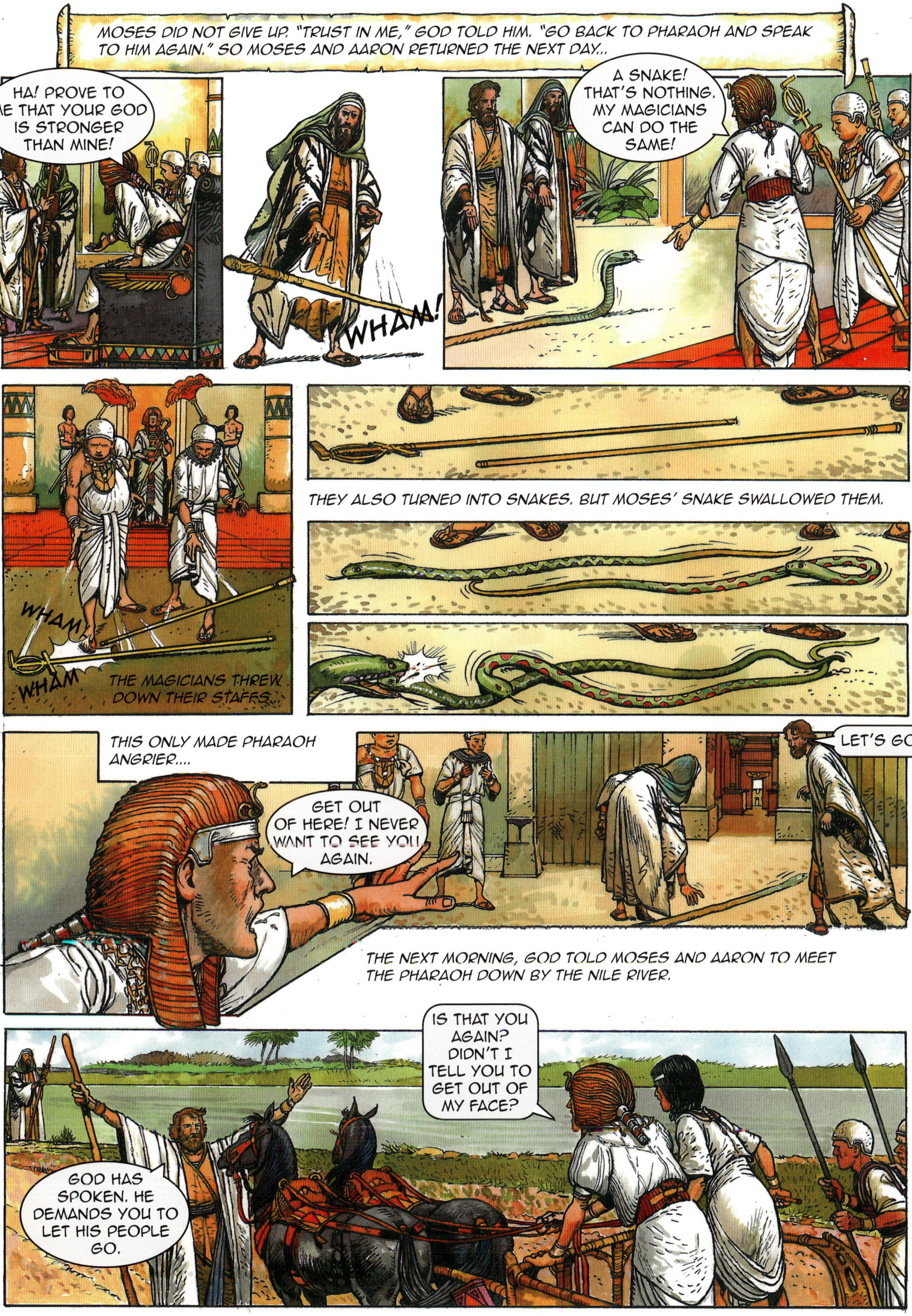
MOSES DID NOT GIVE UP. "TRUST IN ME," GOD TOLD HIM. "GO BACK TO PHARAOH AND SPEAK TO HIM AGAIN." SO MOSES AND AARON RETURNED THE NEXT DAY...
HA! PROVE TO ME THAT YOUR GOD IS STRONGER THAN MINE!
WHAM!
A SNAKE! THAT'S NOTHING. MY MAGICIANS CAN DO THE SAME!
WHAM
WHAM
THE MAGICIANS THREW DOWN THEIR STAFFS...
THEY ALSO TURNED INTO SNAKES. BUT MOSES' SNAKE SWALLOWED THEM.
THIS ONLY MADE PHARAOH ANGRIER....
GET OUT OF HERE! I NEVER WANT TO SEE YOU AGAIN.
LET'S GO.
THE NEXT MORNING, GOD TOLD MOSES AND AARON TO MEET THE PHARAOH DOWN BY THE NILE RIVER.
IS THAT YOU AGAIN? DIDN'T I TELL YOU TO GET OUT OF MY FACE?
GOD HAS SPOKEN. HE DEMANDS YOU TO LET HIS PEOPLE GO.

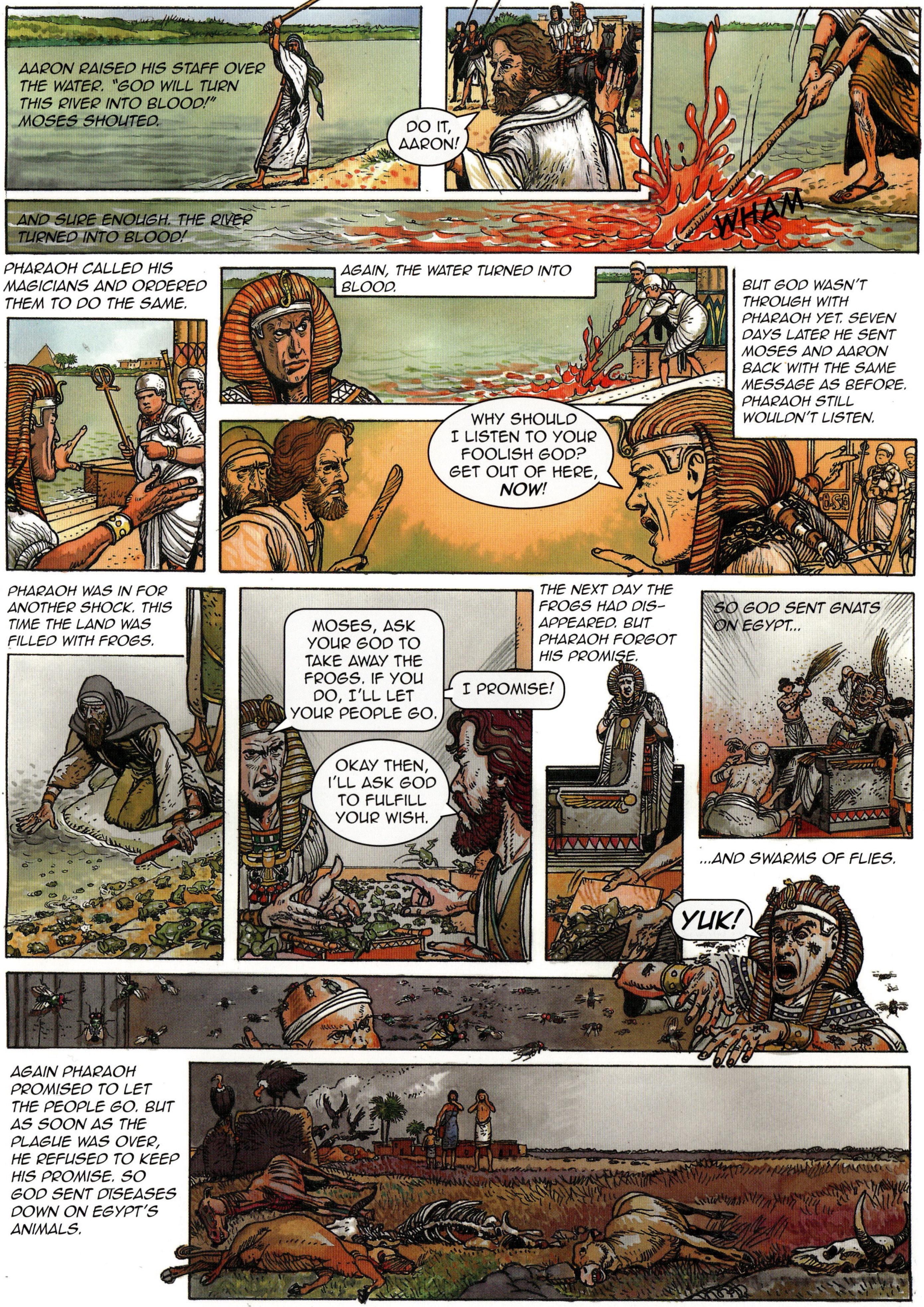
AARON RAISED HIS STAFF OVER THE WATER. "GOD WILL TURN THIS RIVER INTO BLOOD!" MOSES SHOUTED.
DO IT, AARON!
AND SURE ENOUGH, THE RIVER TURNED INTO BLOOD!
WHAM
PHARAOH CALLED HIS MAGICIANS AND ORDERED THEM TO DO THE SAME.
AGAIN, THE WATER TURNED INTO BLOOD.
BUT GOD WASN'T THROUGH WITH PHARAOH YET. SEVEN DAYS LATER HE SENT MOSES AND AARON BACK WITH THE SAME MESSAGE AS BEFORE. PHARAOH STILL WOULDN'T LISTEN.
WHY SHOULD I LISTEN TO YOUR FOOLISH GOD? GET OUT OF HERE, NOW!
PHARAOH WAS IN FOR ANOTHER SHOCK. THIS TIME THE LAND WAS FILLED WITH FROGS.
MOSES, ASK YOUR GOD TO TAKE AWAY THE FROGS. IF YOU DO, I'LL LET YOUR PEOPLE GO.
I PROMISE!
OKAY THEN, I'LL ASK GOD TO FULFILL YOUR WISH.
THE NEXT DAY THE FROGS HAD DIS-APPEARED. BUT PHARAOH FORGOT HIS PROMISE.
SO GOD SENT GNATS ON EGYPT...
...AND SWARMS OF FLIES.
YUK!
AGAIN PHARAOH PROMISED TO LET THE PEOPLE GO. BUT AS SOON AS THE PLAGUE WAS OVER, HE REFUSED TO KEEP HIS PROMISE. SO GOD SENT DISEASES DOWN ON EGYPT'S ANIMALS.

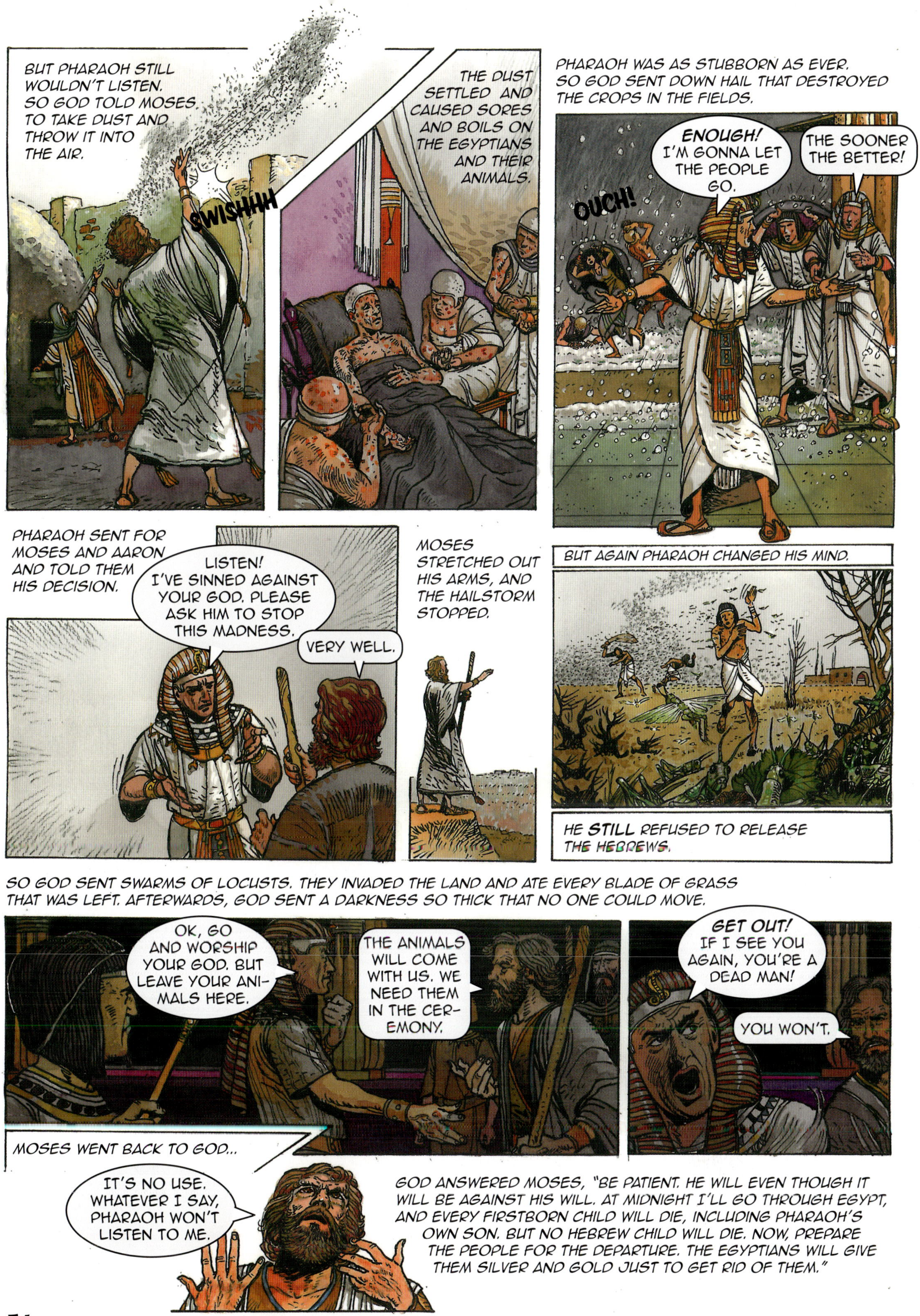
BUT PHARAOH STILL WOULDN'T LISTEN. SO GOD TOLD MOSES TO TAKE DUST AND THROW IT INTO THE AIR.
SWISHHH
THE DUST SETTLED AND CAUSED SORES AND BOILS ON THE EGYPTIANS AND THEIR ANIMALS.
PHARAOH WAS AS STUBBORN AS EVER. SO GOD SENT DOWN HAIL THAT DESTROYED THE CROPS IN THE FIELDS.
OUCH!
ENOUGH! I'M GONNA LET THE PEOPLE GO.
THE SOONER THE BETTER!
PHARAOH SENT FOR MOSES AND AARON AND TOLD THEM HIS DECISION.
LISTEN! I'VE SINNED AGAINST YOUR GOD. PLEASE ASK HIM TO STOP THIS MADNESS.
VERY WELL.
MOSES STRETCHED OUT HIS ARMS, AND THE HAILSTORM STOPPED.
BUT AGAIN PHARAOH CHANGED HIS MIND.
HE STILL REFUSED TO RELEASE THE HEBREWS.
SO GOD SENT SWARMS OF LOCUSTS. THEY INVADED THE LAND AND ATE EVERY BLADE OF GRASS THAT WAS LEFT. AFTERWARDS, GOD SENT A DARKNESS SO THICK THAT NO ONE COULD MOVE.
OK, GO AND WORSHIP YOUR GOD. BUT LEAVE YOUR ANIMALS HERE.
THE ANIMALS WILL COME WITH US. WE NEED THEM IN THE CEREMONY.
GET OUT! IF I SEE YOU AGAIN, YOU'RE A DEAD MAN!
YOU WON'T.
MOSES WENT BACK TO GOD...
IT'S NO USE. WHATEVER I SAY, PHARAOH WON'T LISTEN TO ME.
GOD ANSWERED MOSES, "BE PATIENT. HE WILL EVEN THOUGH IT WILL BE AGAINST HIS WILL. AT MIDNIGHT I'LL GO THROUGH EGYPT, AND EVERY FIRSTBORN CHILD WILL DIE, INCLUDING PHARAOH'S OWN SON. BUT NO HEBREW CHILD WILL DIE. NOW, PREPARE THE PEOPLE FOR THE DEPARTURE. THE EGYPTIANS WILL GIVE THEM SILVER AND GOLD JUST TO GET RID OF THEM."

THE NEXT DAY MOSES GATHERED THE HEBREWS TOGETHER...
GO HOME AND PACK. IT'S TIME TO LEAVE!
BUT FIRST TAKE A LAMB AMONG YOUR ANIMALS, KILL IT, AND EAT THE PASSOVER MEAL TO HONOR OUR GOD. BUT EAT IT QUICKLY.
MOSES TOLD THE ISRAELITES TO TAKE THE BLOOD FROM THE LAMB AND SMEAR IT ON THEIR DOORPOSTS. THE ANGEL OF DEATH WOULD SEE THE BLOOD AND PASS BY.
SO THE ISRAELITES GOT FULLY DRESSED, TIED THEIR SANDALS ON THEIR FEET, AND ATE WITH THEIR STAFF IN HAND.
THAT NIGHT, WHEN THE ANGEL OF DEATH WENT THROUGH EGYPT, THE ISRAELITES WERE SAFE.
BUT EVERY FIRSTBORN CHILD OF EGYPTIAN PARENTS DIED, AND A GREAT CRY OF WAILING AND LAMENT WAS HEARD THROUGHOUT EGYPT.
GOD TOLD MOSES TO ALWAYS REMEMBER THE NIGHT WHEN HE SAVED HIS PEOPLE FROM DEATH AND LED THEM OUT OF EGYPT.
MY SON! I LOVED YOU, AND NOW YOU'RE DEAD. MAY GOD HAVE MERCY ON ME.

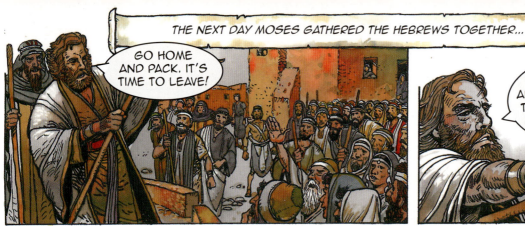

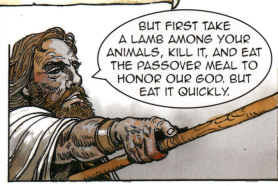

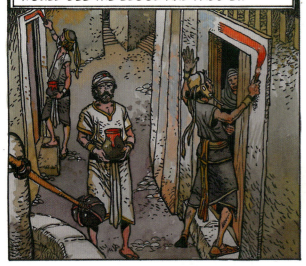

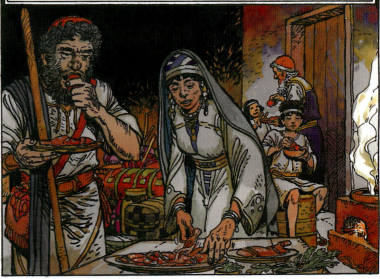

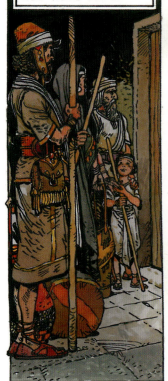

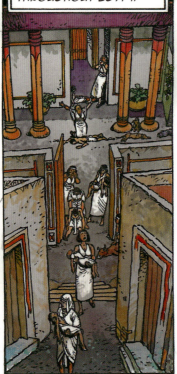

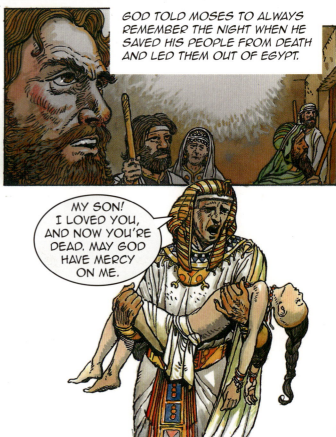

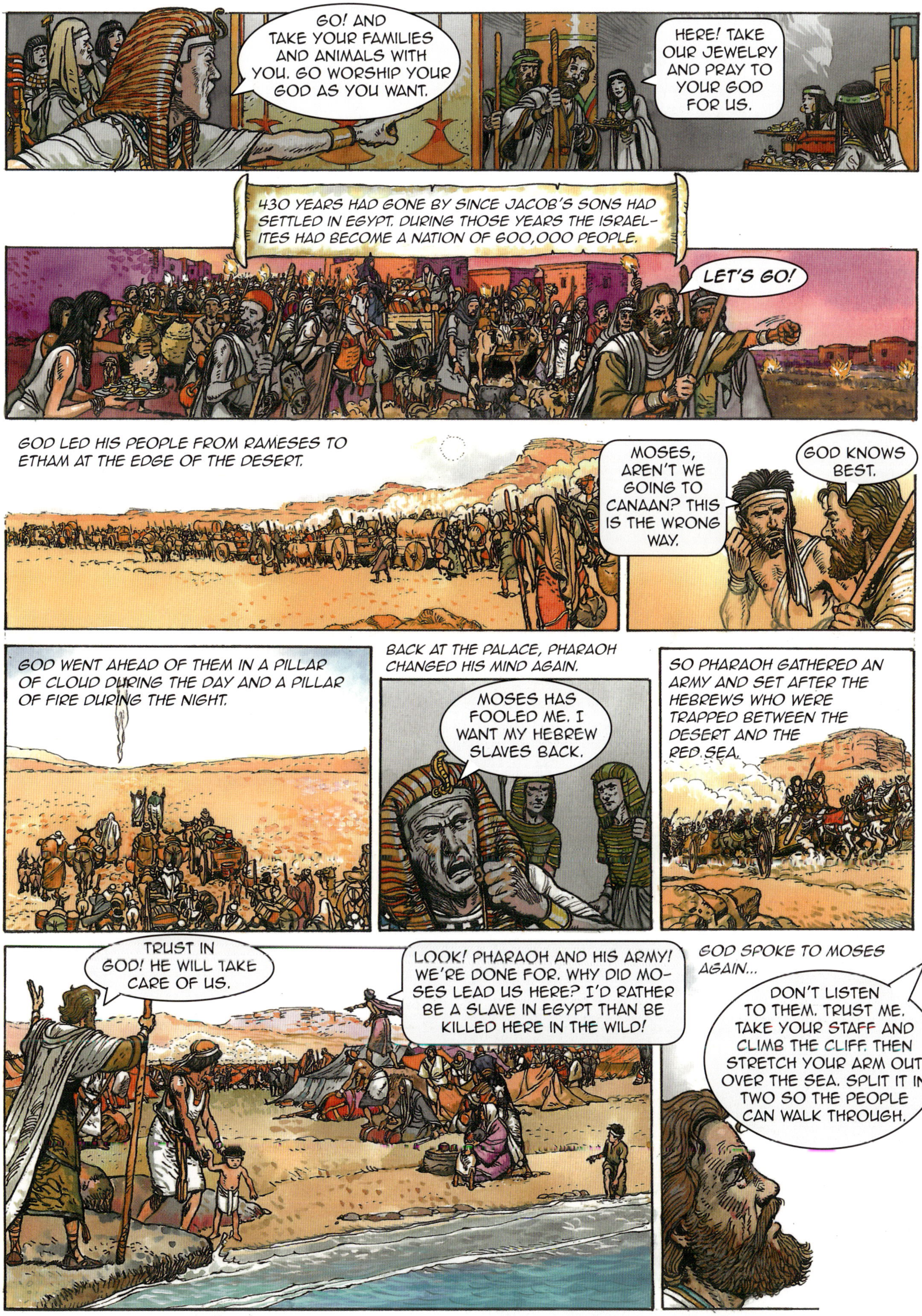
GO! AND TAKE YOUR FAMILIES AND ANIMALS WITH YOU. GO WORSHIP YOUR GOD AS YOU WANT.
HERE! TAKE OUR JEWELRY AND PRAY TO YOUR GOD FOR US.
430 YEARS HAD GONE BY SINCE JACOB'S SONS HAD SETTLED IN EGYPT. DURING THOSE YEARS THE ISRAELITES HAD BECOME A NATION OF 600,000 PEOPLE.
LET'S GO!
GOD LED HIS PEOPLE FROM RAMESES TO ETHAM AT THE EDGE OF THE DESERT.
MOSES, AREN'T WE GOING TO CANAAN? THIS IS THE WRONG WAY.
GOD KNOWS BEST.
GOD WENT AHEAD OF THEM IN A PILLAR OF CLOUD DURING THE DAY AND A PILLAR OF FIRE DURING THE NIGHT.
BACK AT THE PALACE, PHARAOH CHANGED HIS MIND AGAIN.
MOSES HAS FOOLED ME. I WANT MY HEBREW SLAVES BACK.
SO PHARAOH GATHERED AN ARMY AND SET AFTER THE HEBREWS WHO WERE TRAPPED BETWEEN THE DESERT AND THE RED SEA.
TRUST IN GOD! HE WILL TAKE CARE OF US.
LOOK! PHARAOH AND HIS ARMY! WE'RE DONE FOR. WHY DID MOSES LEAD US HERE? I'D RATHER BE A SLAVE IN EGYPT THAN BE KILLED HERE IN THE WILD!
GOD SPOKE TO MOSES AGAIN...
DON'T LISTEN TO THEM. TRUST ME. TAKE YOUR STAFF AND CLIMB THE CLIFF. THEN STRETCH YOUR ARM OUT OVER THE SEA. SPLIT IT IN TWO SO THE PEOPLE CAN WALK THROUGH.

MOSES DID EXACTLY AS GOD HAD TOLD HIM. SOON A MIGHTY EAST WIND SWEPT OVER THE DESERT AND MADE THE SEA PART.

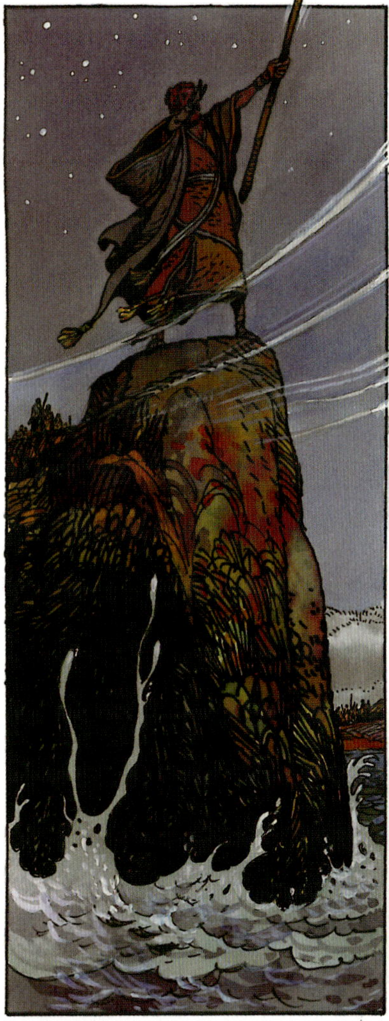

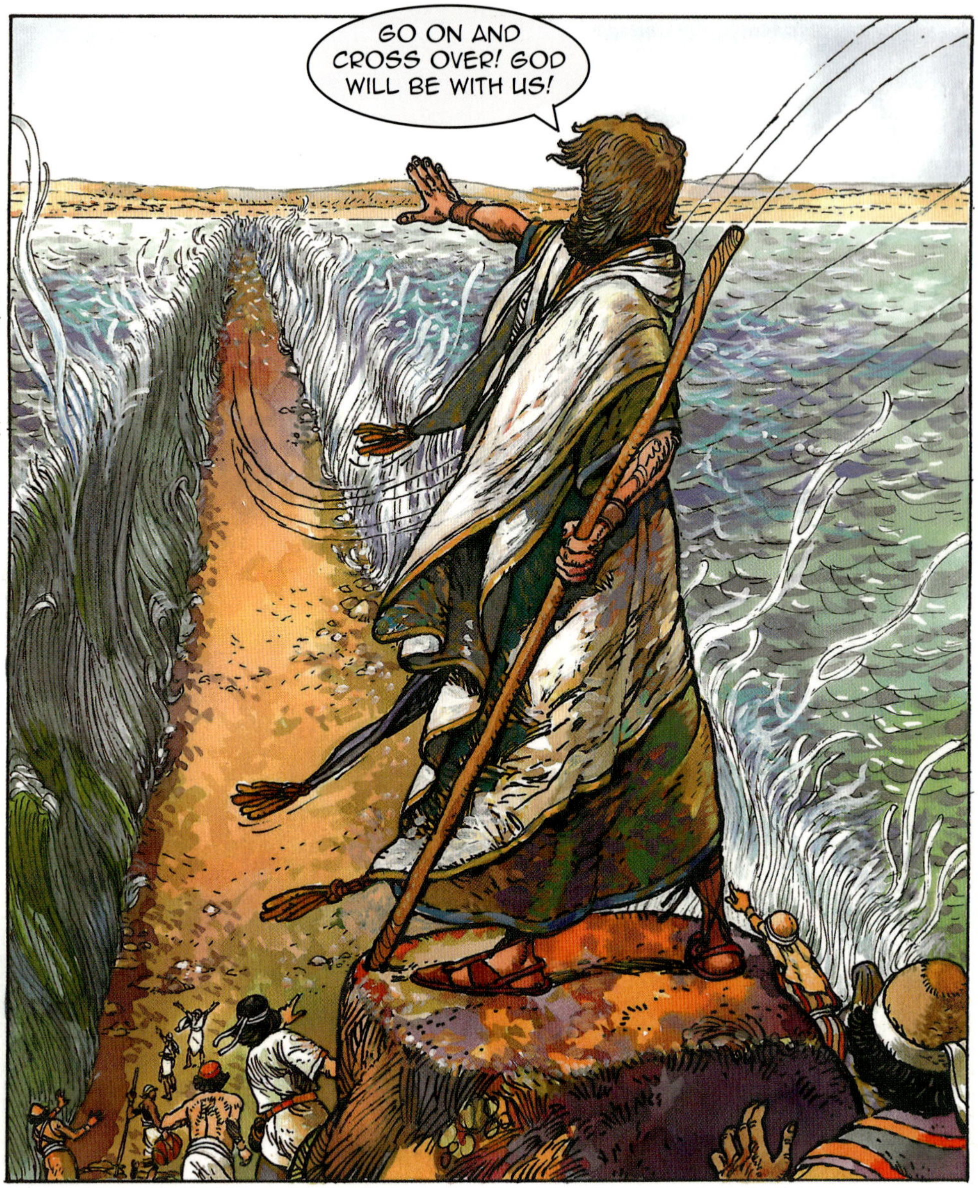
GO ON AND CROSS OVER! GOD WILL BE WITH US!

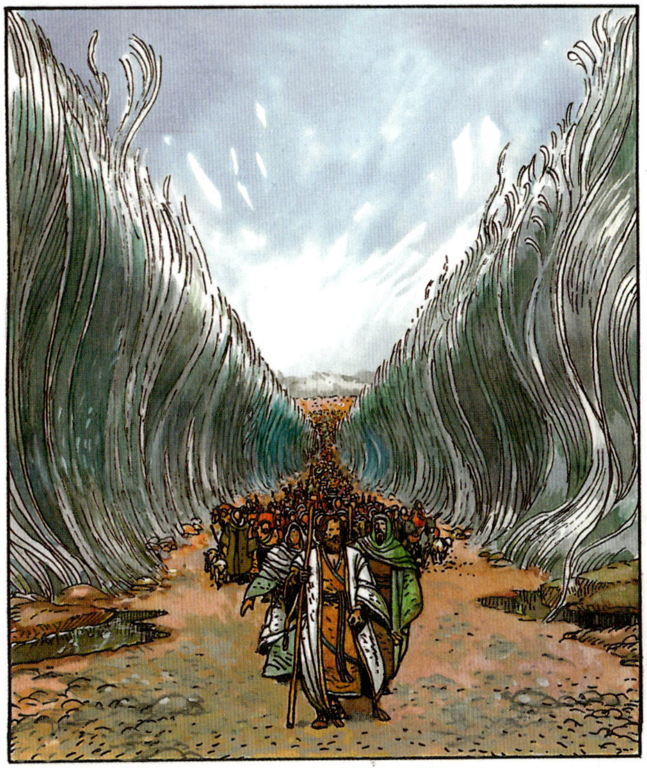

THE ISRAELITES HURRIED ACROSS THE SEABED WITH THE EGYPTIANS ON THEIR HEELS. BUT GOD CAUSED THE EGYPTIANS TO PANIC AS THEIR CHARIOT WHEELS SUNK IN THE WET SAND.

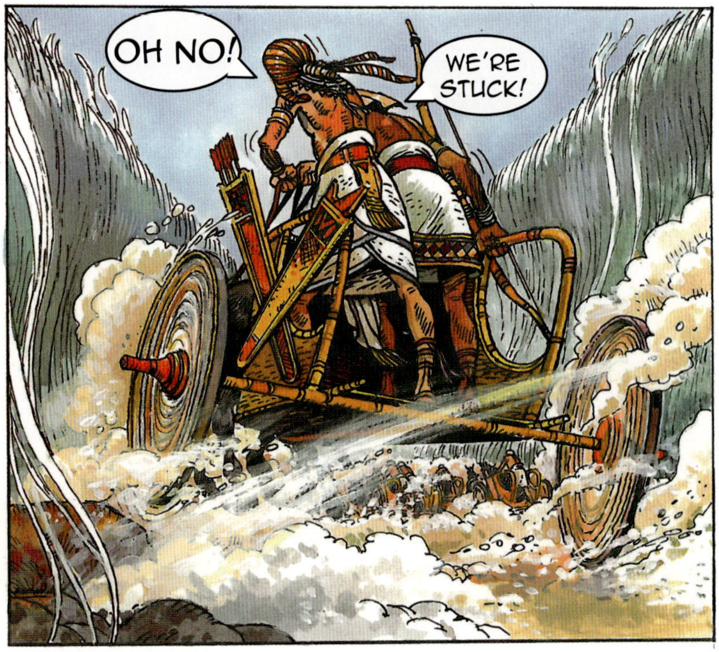
OH NO!
WE'RE STUCK!

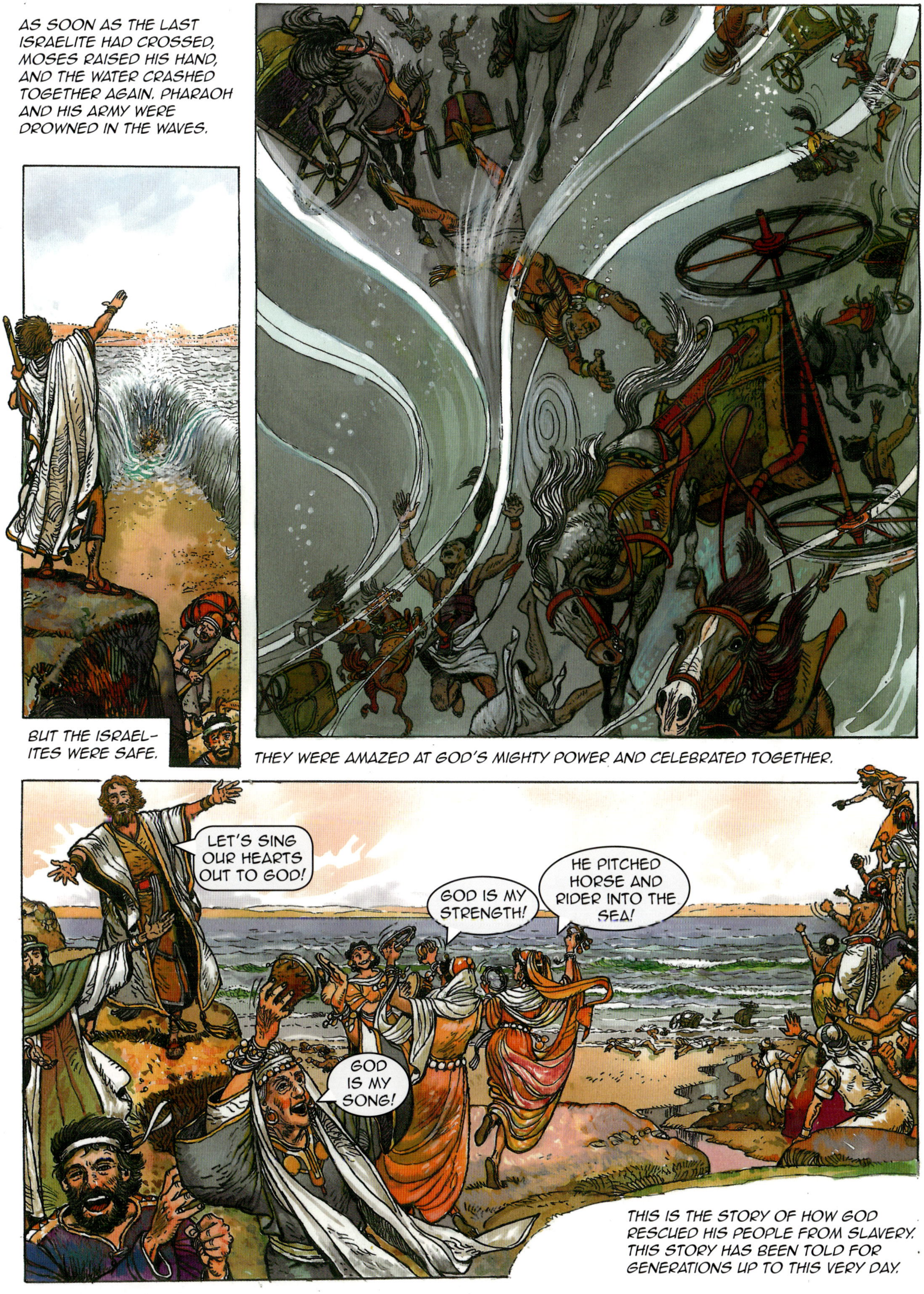
AS SOON AS THE LAST ISRAELITE HAD CROSSED, MOSES RAISED HIS HAND, AND THE WATER CRASHED TOGETHER AGAIN. PHARAOH AND HIS ARMY WERE DROWNED IN THE WAVES.
BUT THE ISRAEL-ITES WERE SAFE.
THEY WERE AMAZED AT GOD'S MIGHTY POWER AND CELEBRATED TOGETHER.
LET'S SING OUR HEARTS OUT TO GOD!
GOD IS MY STRENGTH!
HE PITCHED HORSE AND RIDER INTO THE SEA!
GOD IS MY SONG!
THIS IS THE STORY OF HOW GOD RESCUED HIS PEOPLE FROM SLAVERY. THIS STORY HAS BEEN TOLD FOR GENERATIONS UP TO THIS VERY DAY.

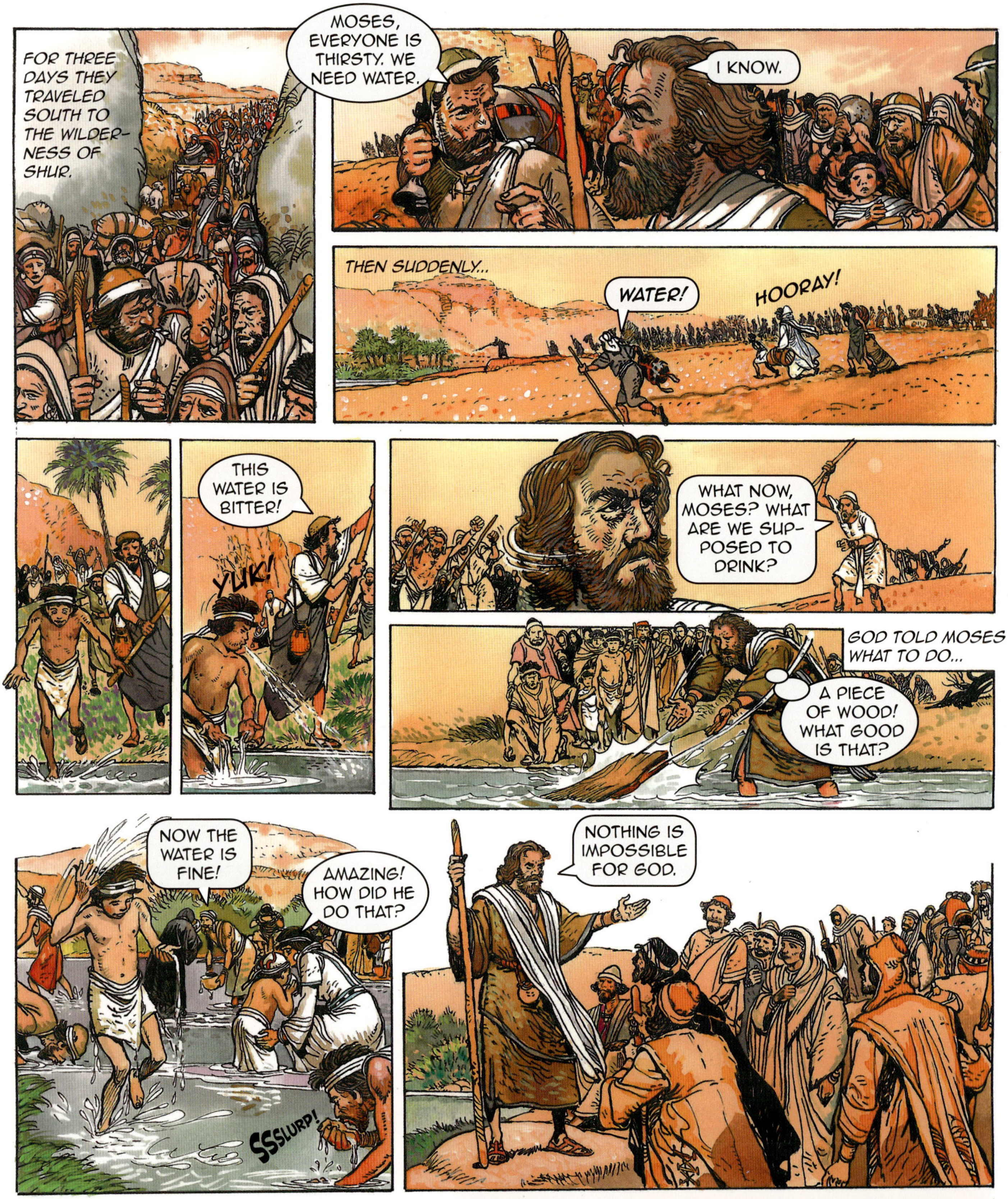
FOR THREE DAYS THEY TRAVELED SOUTH TO THE WILDERNESS OF SHUR.
MOSES, EVERYONE IS THIRSTY. WE NEED WATER.
I KNOW.
THEN SUDDENLY...
WATER!
HOORAY!
THIS WATER IS BITTER!
YUK!
WHAT NOW, MOSES? WHAT ARE WE SUPPOSED TO DRINK?
GOD TOLD MOSES WHAT TO DO...
A PIECE OF WOOD! WHAT GOOD IS THAT?
NOW THE WATER IS FINE!
AMAZING! HOW DID HE DO THAT?
SSSLURP!
NOTHING IS IMPOSSIBLE FOR GOD.

GOD SAID TO MOSES, "IF YOU LISTEN CAREFULLY TO ME AND OBEY MY WORD, I'LL CERTAINLY NOT SMITE YOU WITH DISEASE LIKE I DID THE EGYPTIANS. I'LL TAKE CARE OF YOU. I'LL BE YOUR HEALER."

THE PEOPLE TRAVELED ON, AND THEY BELIEVED GOD WOULD PROVIDE FOR THEM IN THE WILDERNESS. HE CERTAINLY DID. THEY SET UP CAMP AT ELIM -- AN OASIS WITH TWELVE SPRINGS OF WATER AND 70 PALM TREES AROUND.

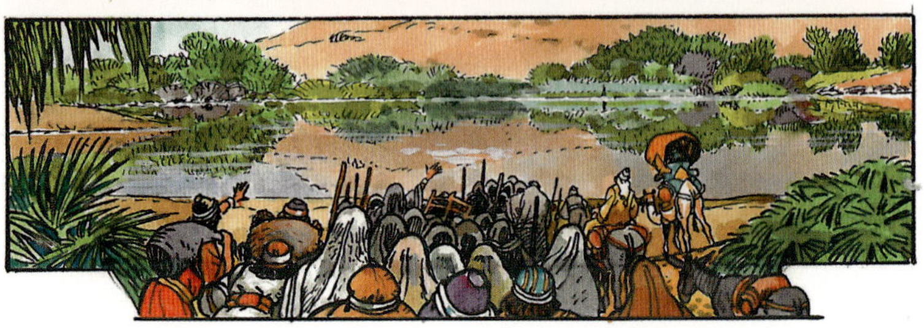

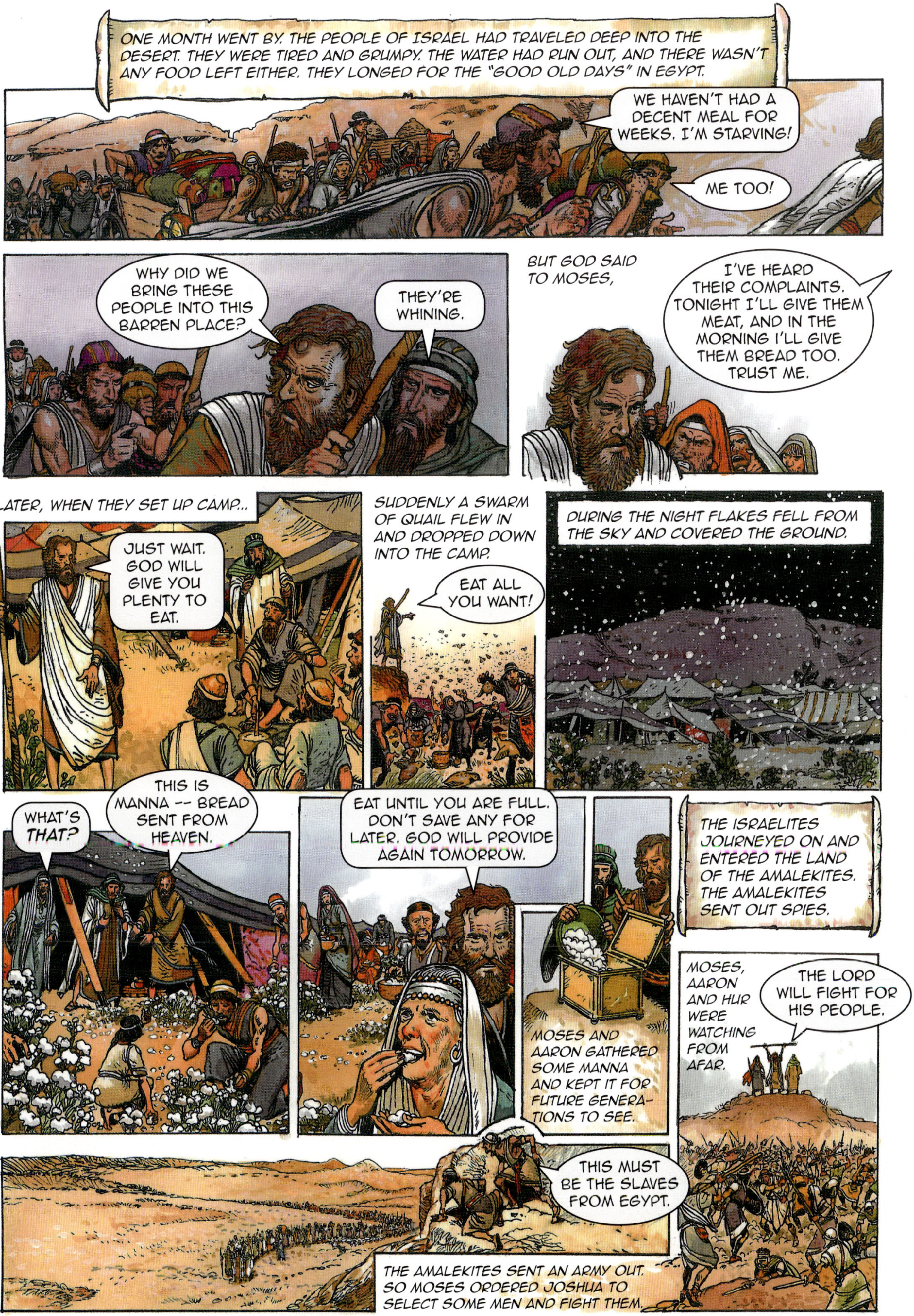

ONE MONTH WENT BY. THE PEOPLE OF ISRAEL HAD TRAVELED DEEP INTO THE DESERT. THEY WERE TIRED AND GRUMPY. THE WATER HAD RUN OUT, AND THERE WASN'T ANY FOOD LEFT EITHER. THEY LONGED FOR THE "GOOD OLD DAYS" IN EGYPT.
WE HAVEN'T HAD A DECENT MEAL FOR WEEKS. I'M STARVING!
ME TOO!
WHY DID WE BRING THESE PEOPLE INTO THIS BARREN PLACE?
THEY'RE WHINING.
BUT GOD SAID TO MOSES,
I'VE HEARD THEIR COMPLAINTS. TONIGHT I'LL GIVE THEM MEAT, AND IN THE MORNING I'LL GIVE THEM BREAD TOO. TRUST ME.
LATER, WHEN THEY SET UP CAMP...
JUST WAIT. GOD WILL GIVE YOU PLENTY TO EAT.
SUDDENLY A SWARM OF QUAIL FLEW IN AND DROPPED DOWN INTO THE CAMP.
EAT ALL YOU WANT!
DURING THE NIGHT FLAKES FELL FROM THE SKY AND COVERED THE GROUND.
WHAT'S *THAT?*
THIS IS MANNA -- BREAD SENT FROM HEAVEN.
EAT UNTIL YOU ARE FULL. DON'T SAVE ANY FOR LATER. GOD WILL PROVIDE AGAIN TOMORROW.
MOSES AND AARON GATHERED SOME MANNA AND KEPT IT FOR FUTURE GENERATIONS TO SEE.
THE ISRAELITES JOURNEYED ON AND ENTERED THE LAND OF THE AMALEKITES. THE AMALEKITES SENT OUT SPIES.
MOSES, AARON AND HUR WERE WATCHING FROM AFAR.
THE LORD WILL FIGHT FOR HIS PEOPLE.
THIS MUST BE THE SLAVES FROM EGYPT.
THE AMALEKITES SENT AN ARMY OUT. SO MOSES ORDERED JOSHUA TO SELECT SOME MEN AND FIGHT THEM.

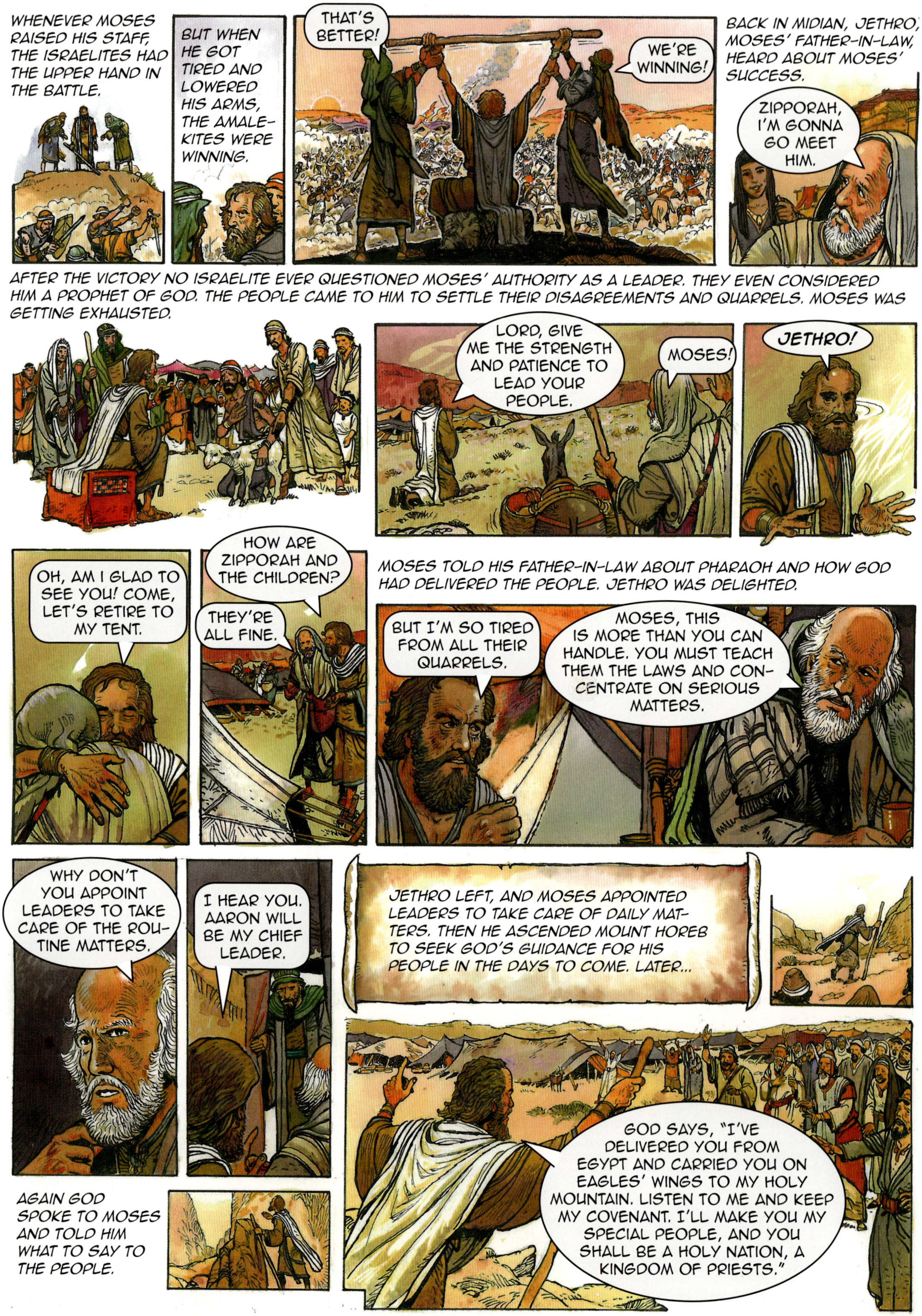

WHENEVER MOSES RAISED HIS STAFF, THE ISRAELITES HAD THE UPPER HAND IN THE BATTLE.
BUT WHEN HE GOT TIRED AND LOWERED HIS ARMS, THE AMALEKITES WERE WINNING.
THAT'S BETTER!
WE'RE WINNING!
BACK IN MIDIAN, JETHRO, MOSES' FATHER-IN-LAW, HEARD ABOUT MOSES' SUCCESS.
ZIPPORAH, I'M GONNA GO MEET HIM.
AFTER THE VICTORY NO ISRAELITE EVER QUESTIONED MOSES' AUTHORITY AS A LEADER. THEY EVEN CONSIDERED HIM A PROPHET OF GOD. THE PEOPLE CAME TO HIM TO SETTLE THEIR DISAGREEMENTS AND QUARRELS. MOSES WAS GETTING EXHAUSTED.
LORD, GIVE ME THE STRENGTH AND PATIENCE TO LEAD YOUR PEOPLE.
MOSES!
JETHRO!
OH, AM I GLAD TO SEE YOU! COME, LET'S RETIRE TO MY TENT.
HOW ARE ZIPPORAH AND THE CHILDREN?
THEY'RE ALL FINE.
MOSES TOLD HIS FATHER-IN-LAW ABOUT PHARAOH AND HOW GOD HAD DELIVERED THE PEOPLE. JETHRO WAS DELIGHTED.
BUT I'M SO TIRED FROM ALL THEIR QUARRELS.
MOSES, THIS IS MORE THAN YOU CAN HANDLE. YOU MUST TEACH THEM THE LAWS AND CONCENTRATE ON SERIOUS MATTERS.
WHY DON'T YOU APPOINT LEADERS TO TAKE CARE OF THE ROUTINE MATTERS.
I HEAR YOU. AARON WILL BE MY CHIEF LEADER.
JETHRO LEFT, AND MOSES APPOINTED LEADERS TO TAKE CARE OF DAILY MATTERS. THEN HE ASCENDED MOUNT HOREB TO SEEK GOD'S GUIDANCE FOR HIS PEOPLE IN THE DAYS TO COME. LATER...
AGAIN GOD SPOKE TO MOSES AND TOLD HIM WHAT TO SAY TO THE PEOPLE.
GOD SAYS, "I'VE DELIVERED YOU FROM EGYPT AND CARRIED YOU ON EAGLES' WINGS TO MY HOLY MOUNTAIN. LISTEN TO ME AND KEEP MY COVENANT. I'LL MAKE YOU MY SPECIAL PEOPLE, AND YOU SHALL BE A HOLY NATION, A KINGDOM OF PRIESTS."

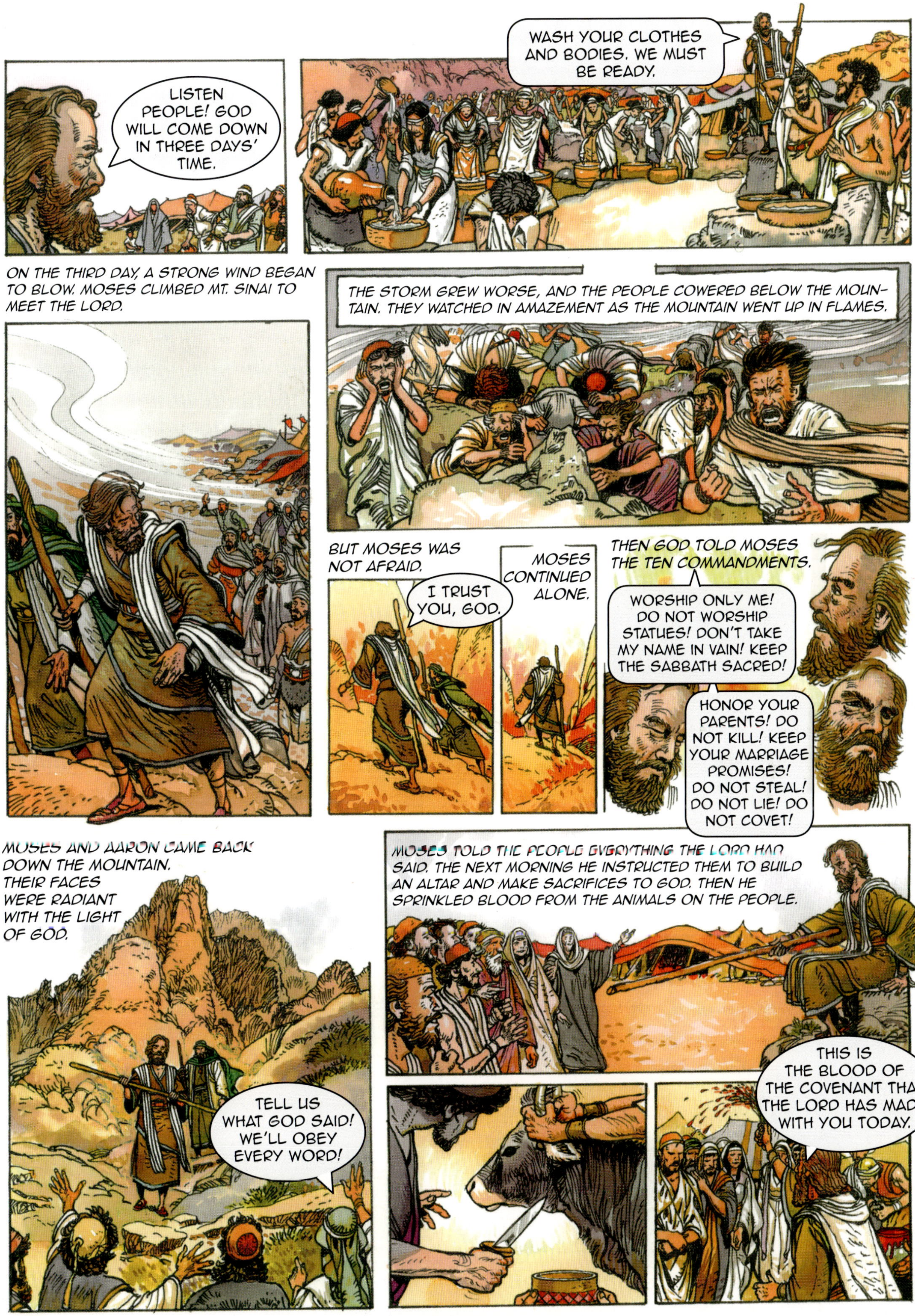
LISTEN PEOPLE! GOD WILL COME DOWN IN THREE DAYS' TIME.
WASH YOUR CLOTHES AND BODIES. WE MUST BE READY.
ON THE THIRD DAY, A STRONG WIND BEGAN TO BLOW. MOSES CLIMBED MT. SINAI TO MEET THE LORD.
THE STORM GREW WORSE, AND THE PEOPLE COWERED BELOW THE MOUNTAIN. THEY WATCHED IN AMAZEMENT AS THE MOUNTAIN WENT UP IN FLAMES.
BUT MOSES WAS NOT AFRAID.
I TRUST YOU, GOD.
MOSES CONTINUED ALONE.
THEN GOD TOLD MOSES THE TEN COMMANDMENTS.
WORSHIP ONLY ME! DO NOT WORSHIP STATUES! DON'T TAKE MY NAME IN VAIN! KEEP THE SABBATH SACRED!
HONOR YOUR PARENTS! DO NOT KILL! KEEP YOUR MARRIAGE PROMISES! DO NOT STEAL! DO NOT LIE! DO NOT COVET!
MOSES AND AARON CAME BACK DOWN THE MOUNTAIN. THEIR FACES WERE RADIANT WITH THE LIGHT OF GOD.
TELL US WHAT GOD SAID! WE'LL OBEY EVERY WORD!
MOSES TOLD THE PEOPLE EVERYTHING THE LORD HAD SAID. THE NEXT MORNING HE INSTRUCTED THEM TO BUILD AN ALTAR AND MAKE SACRIFICES TO GOD. THEN HE SPRINKLED BLOOD FROM THE ANIMALS ON THE PEOPLE.
THIS IS THE BLOOD OF THE COVENANT THAT THE LORD HAS MADE WITH YOU TODAY.

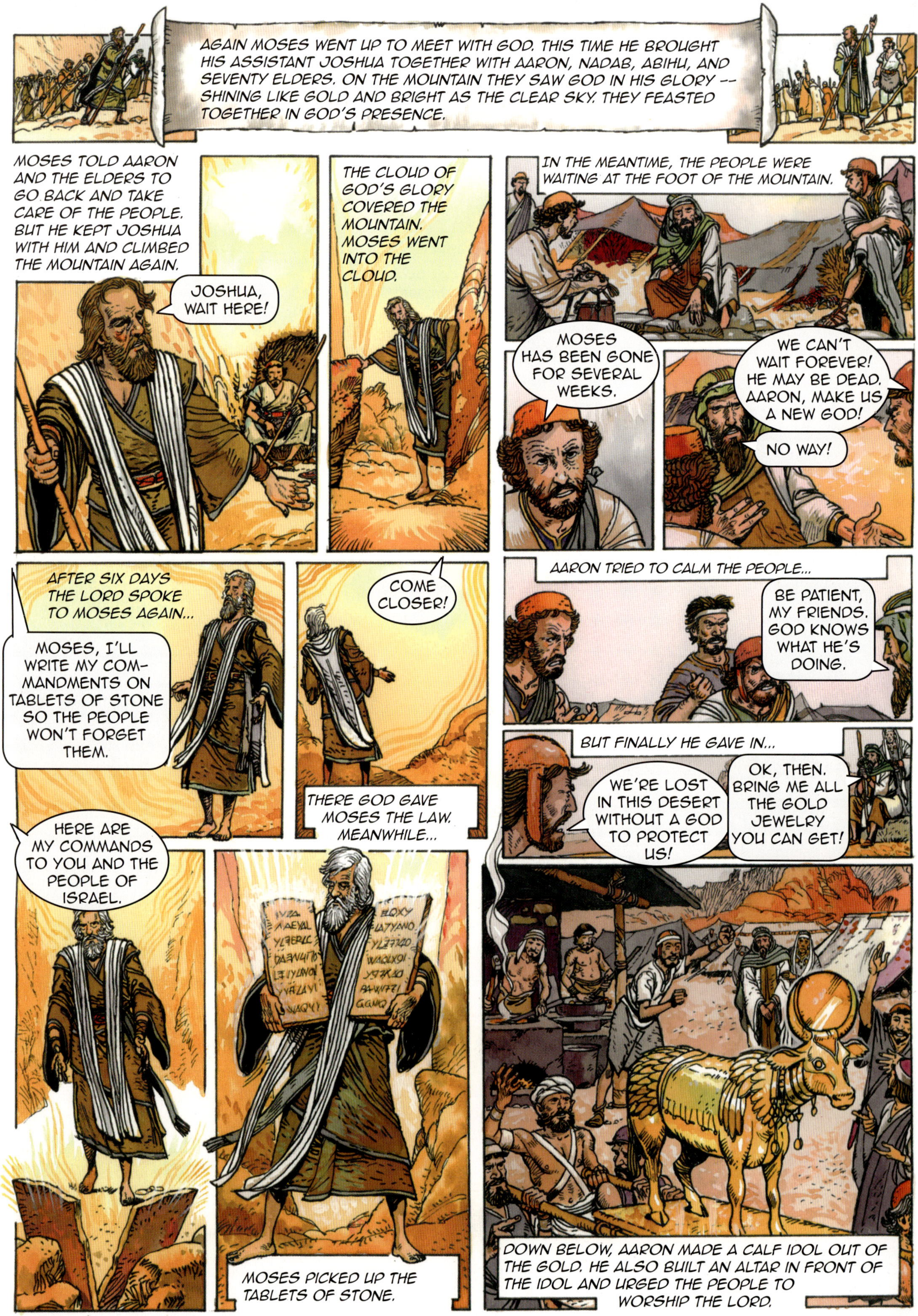
AGAIN MOSES WENT UP TO MEET WITH GOD. THIS TIME HE BROUGHT HIS ASSISTANT JOSHUA TOGETHER WITH AARON, NADAB, ABIHU, AND SEVENTY ELDERS. ON THE MOUNTAIN THEY SAW GOD IN HIS GLORY -- SHINING LIKE GOLD AND BRIGHT AS THE CLEAR SKY. THEY FEASTED TOGETHER IN GOD'S PRESENCE.
MOSES TOLD AARON AND THE ELDERS TO GO BACK AND TAKE CARE OF THE PEOPLE. BUT HE KEPT JOSHUA WITH HIM AND CLIMBED THE MOUNTAIN AGAIN.
JOSHUA, WAIT HERE!
THE CLOUD OF GOD'S GLORY COVERED THE MOUNTAIN. MOSES WENT INTO THE CLOUD.
IN THE MEANTIME, THE PEOPLE WERE WAITING AT THE FOOT OF THE MOUNTAIN.
MOSES HAS BEEN GONE FOR SEVERAL WEEKS.
WE CAN'T WAIT FOREVER! HE MAY BE DEAD. AARON, MAKE US A NEW GOD!
NO WAY!
AFTER SIX DAYS THE LORD SPOKE TO MOSES AGAIN...
MOSES, I'LL WRITE MY COMMANDMENTS ON TABLETS OF STONE SO THE PEOPLE WON'T FORGET THEM.
COME CLOSER!
THERE GOD GAVE MOSES THE LAW. MEANWHILE...
AARON TRIED TO CALM THE PEOPLE...
BE PATIENT, MY FRIENDS. GOD KNOWS WHAT HE'S DOING.
BUT FINALLY HE GAVE IN...
WE'RE LOST IN THIS DESERT WITHOUT A GOD TO PROTECT US!
OK, THEN. BRING ME ALL THE GOLD JEWELRY YOU CAN GET!
HERE ARE MY COMMANDS TO YOU AND THE PEOPLE OF ISRAEL.
MOSES PICKED UP THE TABLETS OF STONE.
DOWN BELOW, AARON MADE A CALF IDOL OUT OF THE GOLD. HE ALSO BUILT AN ALTAR IN FRONT OF THE IDOL AND URGED THE PEOPLE TO WORSHIP THE LORD.

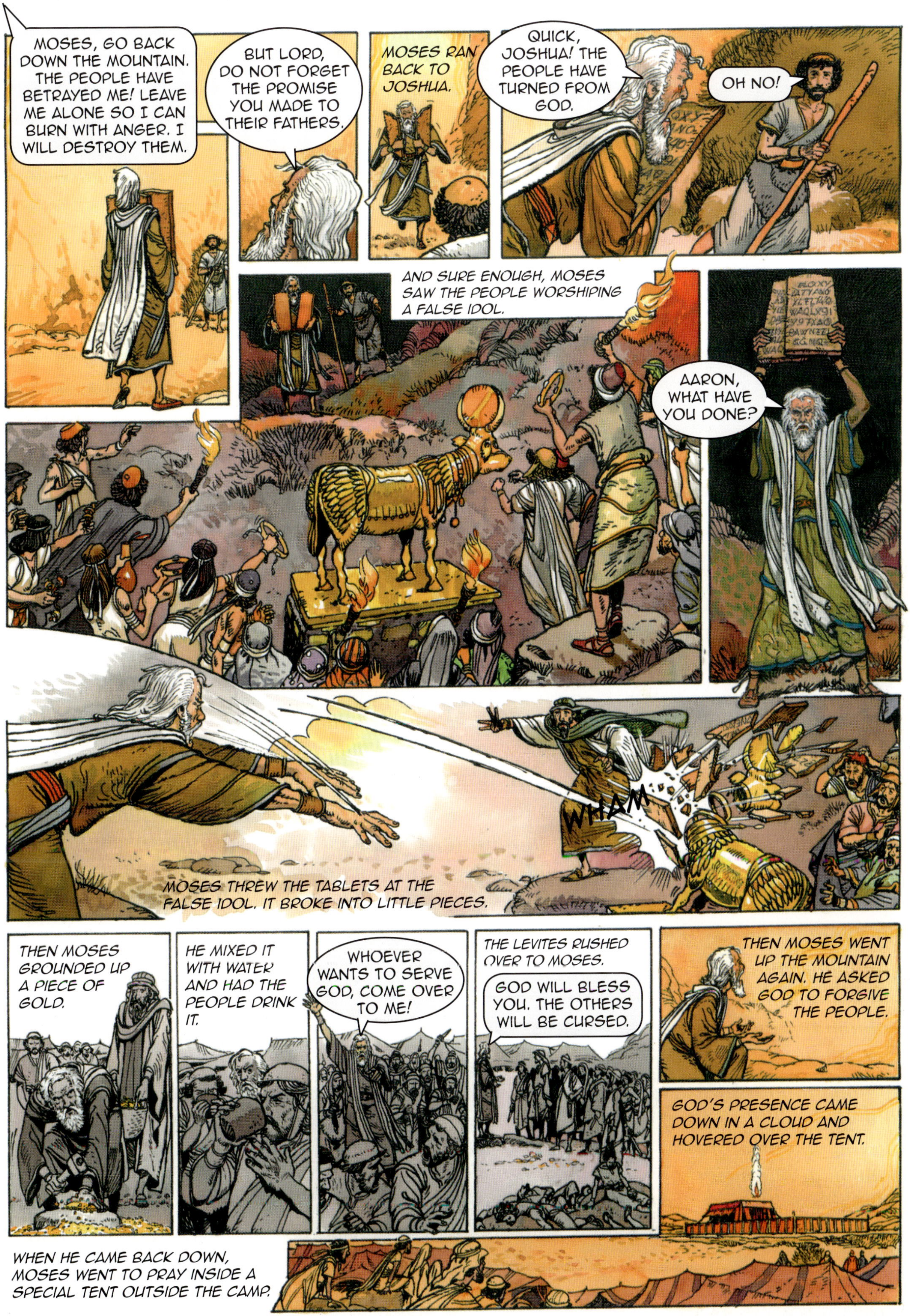
MOSES, GO BACK DOWN THE MOUNTAIN. THE PEOPLE HAVE BETRAYED ME! LEAVE ME ALONE SO I CAN BURN WITH ANGER. I WILL DESTROY THEM.
BUT LORD, DO NOT FORGET THE PROMISE YOU MADE TO THEIR FATHERS.
MOSES RAN BACK TO JOSHUA.
QUICK, JOSHUA! THE PEOPLE HAVE TURNED FROM GOD.
OH NO!
AND SURE ENOUGH, MOSES SAW THE PEOPLE WORSHIPING A FALSE IDOL.
AARON, WHAT HAVE YOU DONE?
WHAM
MOSES THREW THE TABLETS AT THE FALSE IDOL. IT BROKE INTO LITTLE PIECES.
THEN MOSES GROUNDED UP A PIECE OF GOLD.
HE MIXED IT WITH WATER AND HAD THE PEOPLE DRINK IT.
WHOEVER WANTS TO SERVE GOD, COME OVER TO ME!
THE LEVITES RUSHED OVER TO MOSES.
GOD WILL BLESS YOU. THE OTHERS WILL BE CURSED.
THEN MOSES WENT UP THE MOUNTAIN AGAIN. HE ASKED GOD TO FORGIVE THE PEOPLE.
GOD'S PRESENCE CAME DOWN IN A CLOUD AND HOVERED OVER THE TENT.
WHEN HE CAME BACK DOWN, MOSES WENT TO PRAY INSIDE A SPECIAL TENT OUTSIDE THE CAMP.

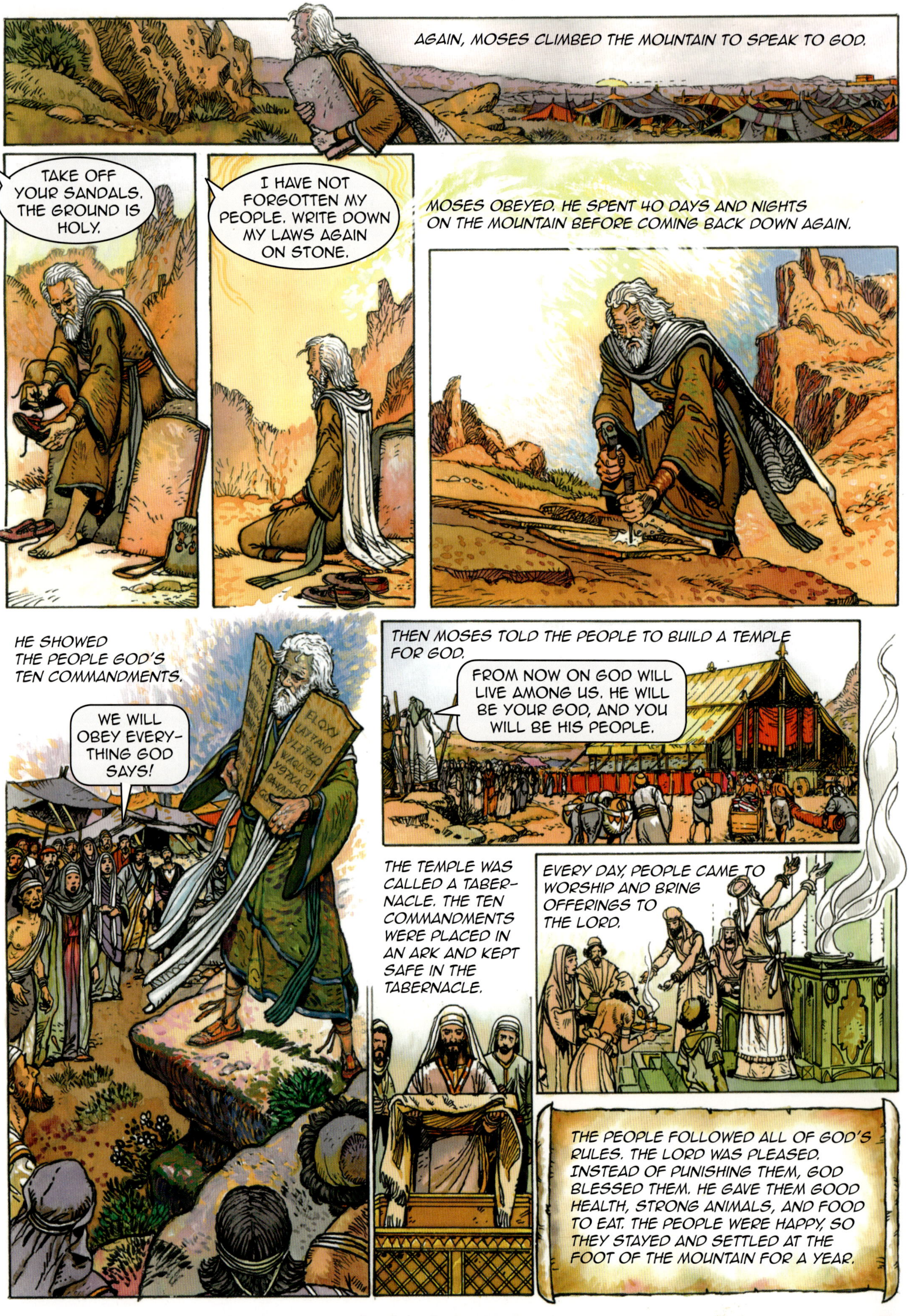
AGAIN, MOSES CLIMBED THE MOUNTAIN TO SPEAK TO GOD.
TAKE OFF YOUR SANDALS. THE GROUND IS HOLY.
I HAVE NOT FORGOTTEN MY PEOPLE. WRITE DOWN MY LAWS AGAIN ON STONE.
MOSES OBEYED. HE SPENT 40 DAYS AND NIGHTS ON THE MOUNTAIN BEFORE COMING BACK DOWN AGAIN.
HE SHOWED THE PEOPLE GOD'S TEN COMMANDMENTS.
WE WILL OBEY EVERYTHING GOD SAYS!
THEN MOSES TOLD THE PEOPLE TO BUILD A TEMPLE FOR GOD.
FROM NOW ON GOD WILL LIVE AMONG US. HE WILL BE YOUR GOD, AND YOU WILL BE HIS PEOPLE.
THE TEMPLE WAS CALLED A TABERNACLE. THE TEN COMMANDMENTS WERE PLACED IN AN ARK AND KEPT SAFE IN THE TABERNACLE.
EVERY DAY, PEOPLE CAME TO WORSHIP AND BRING OFFERINGS TO THE LORD.
THE PEOPLE FOLLOWED ALL OF GOD'S RULES. THE LORD WAS PLEASED. INSTEAD OF PUNISHING THEM, GOD BLESSED THEM. HE GAVE THEM GOOD HEALTH, STRONG ANIMALS, AND FOOD TO EAT. THE PEOPLE WERE HAPPY, SO THEY STAYED AND SETTLED AT THE FOOT OF THE MOUNTAIN FOR A YEAR.

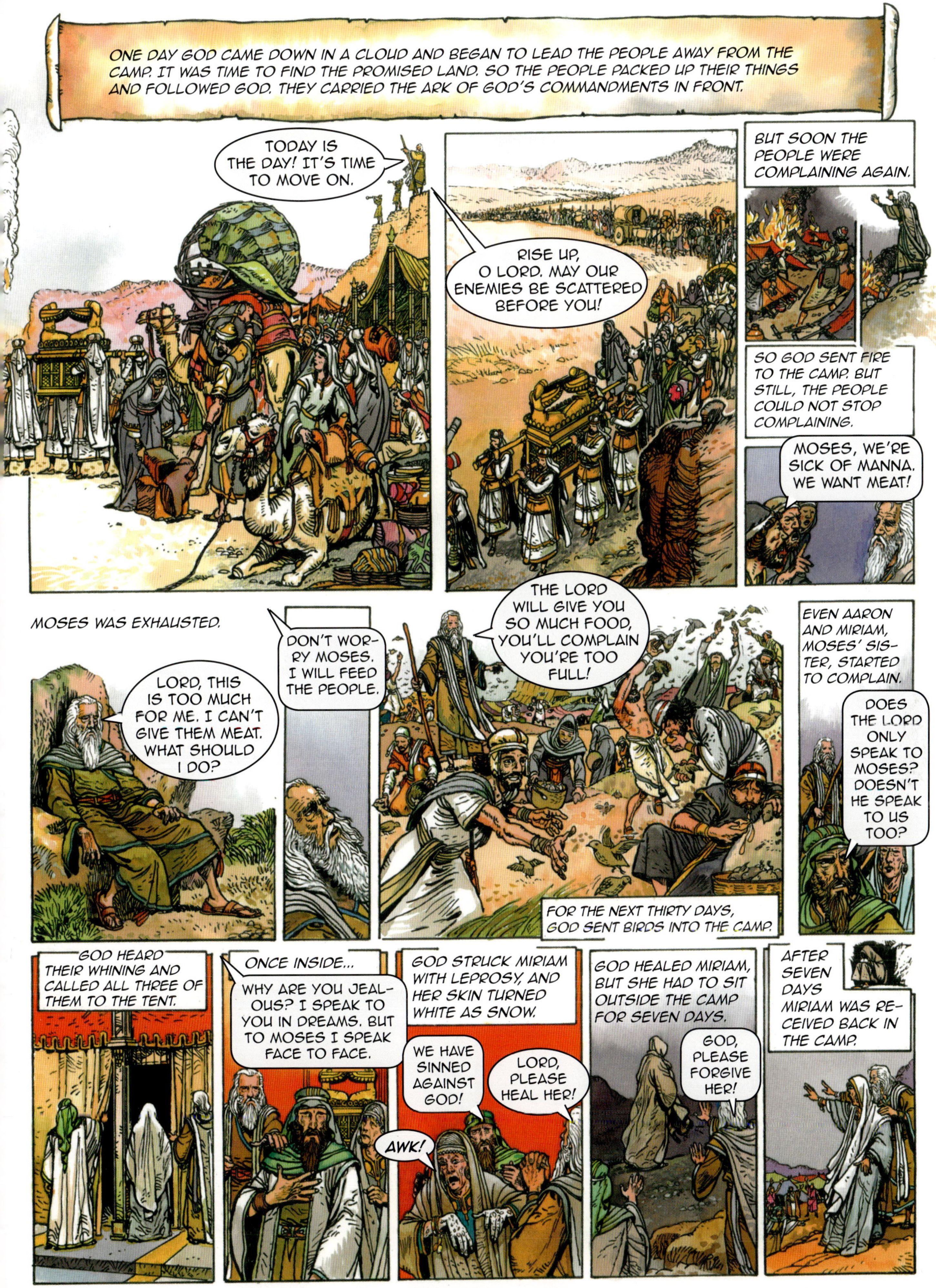

ONE DAY GOD CAME DOWN IN A CLOUD AND BEGAN TO LEAD THE PEOPLE AWAY FROM THE CAMP. IT WAS TIME TO FIND THE PROMISED LAND. SO THE PEOPLE PACKED UP THEIR THINGS AND FOLLOWED GOD. THEY CARRIED THE ARK OF GOD'S COMMANDMENTS IN FRONT.
TODAY IS THE DAY! IT'S TIME TO MOVE ON.
RISE UP, O LORD. MAY OUR ENEMIES BE SCATTERED BEFORE YOU!
BUT SOON THE PEOPLE WERE COMPLAINING AGAIN.
SO GOD SENT FIRE TO THE CAMP. BUT STILL, THE PEOPLE COULD NOT STOP COMPLAINING.
MOSES, WE'RE SICK OF MANNA. WE WANT MEAT!
MOSES WAS EXHAUSTED.
LORD, THIS IS TOO MUCH FOR ME. I CAN'T GIVE THEM MEAT. WHAT SHOULD I DO?
DON'T WORRY MOSES. I WILL FEED THE PEOPLE.
THE LORD WILL GIVE YOU SO MUCH FOOD, YOU'LL COMPLAIN YOU'RE TOO FULL!
FOR THE NEXT THIRTY DAYS, GOD SENT BIRDS INTO THE CAMP.
EVEN AARON AND MIRIAM, MOSES' SISTER, STARTED TO COMPLAIN.
DOES THE LORD ONLY SPEAK TO MOSES? DOESN'T HE SPEAK TO US TOO?
GOD HEARD THEIR WHINING AND CALLED ALL THREE OF THEM TO THE TENT.
ONCE INSIDE...
WHY ARE YOU JEALOUS? I SPEAK TO YOU IN DREAMS. BUT TO MOSES I SPEAK FACE TO FACE.
GOD STRUCK MIRIAM WITH LEPROSY, AND HER SKIN TURNED WHITE AS SNOW.
WE HAVE SINNED AGAINST GOD!
LORD, PLEASE HEAL HER!
AWK!
GOD HEALED MIRIAM, BUT SHE HAD TO SIT OUTSIDE THE CAMP FOR SEVEN DAYS.
GOD, PLEASE FORGIVE HER!
AFTER SEVEN DAYS MIRIAM WAS RECEIVED BACK IN THE CAMP.

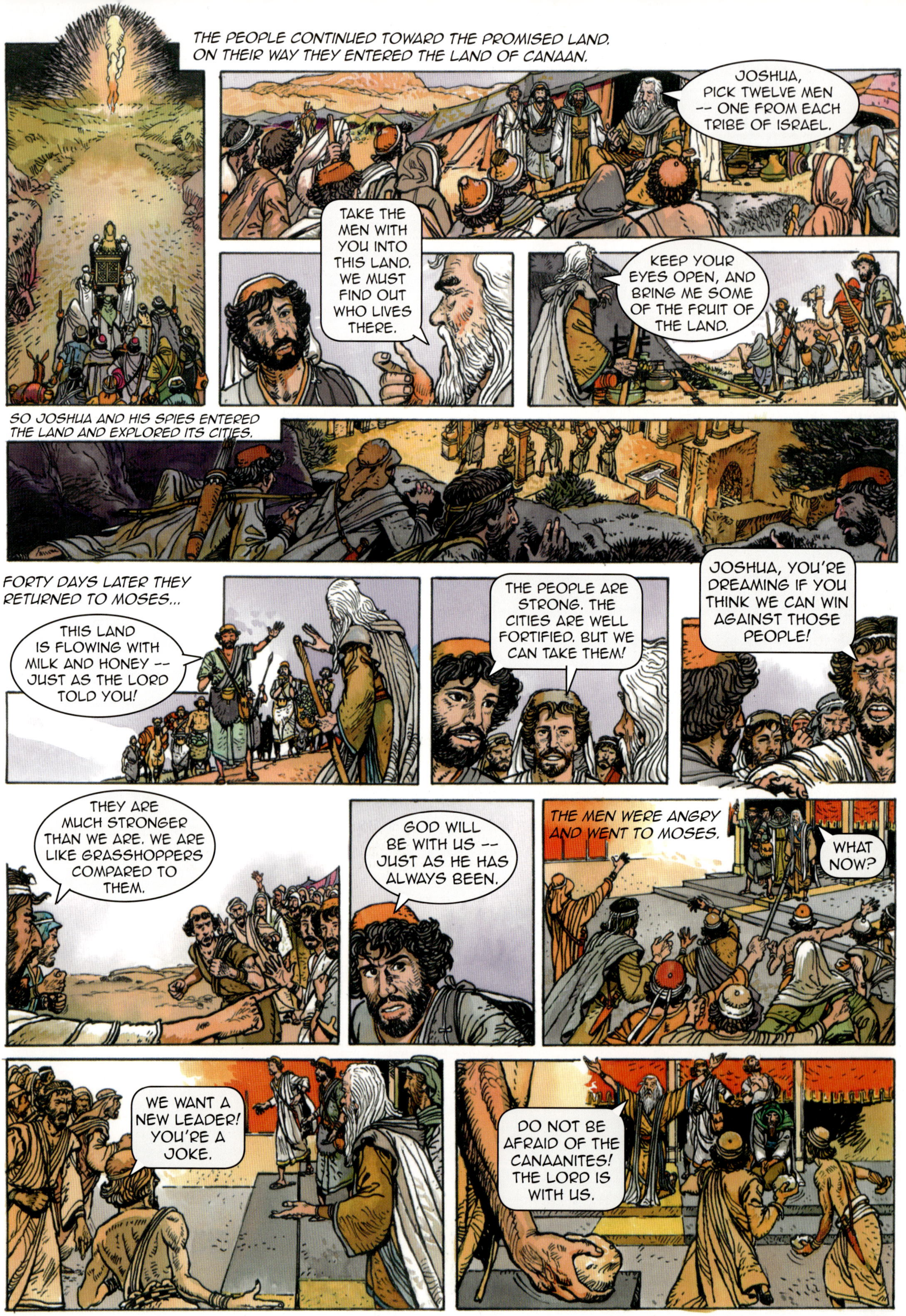
THE PEOPLE CONTINUED TOWARD THE PROMISED LAND. ON THEIR WAY THEY ENTERED THE LAND OF CANAAN.
JOSHUA, PICK TWELVE MEN -- ONE FROM EACH TRIBE OF ISRAEL.
TAKE THE MEN WITH YOU INTO THIS LAND. WE MUST FIND OUT WHO LIVES THERE.
KEEP YOUR EYES OPEN, AND BRING ME SOME OF THE FRUIT OF THE LAND.
SO JOSHUA AND HIS SPIES ENTERED THE LAND AND EXPLORED ITS CITIES.
FORTY DAYS LATER THEY RETURNED TO MOSES...
THIS LAND IS FLOWING WITH MILK AND HONEY -- JUST AS THE LORD TOLD YOU!
THE PEOPLE ARE STRONG. THE CITIES ARE WELL FORTIFIED. BUT WE CAN TAKE THEM!
JOSHUA, YOU'RE DREAMING IF YOU THINK WE CAN WIN AGAINST THOSE PEOPLE!
THEY ARE MUCH STRONGER THAN WE ARE. WE ARE LIKE GRASSHOPPERS COMPARED TO THEM.
GOD WILL BE WITH US -- JUST AS HE HAS ALWAYS BEEN.
THE MEN WERE ANGRY AND WENT TO MOSES.
WHAT NOW?
WE WANT A NEW LEADER! YOU'RE A JOKE.
DO NOT BE AFRAID OF THE CANAANITES! THE LORD IS WITH US.

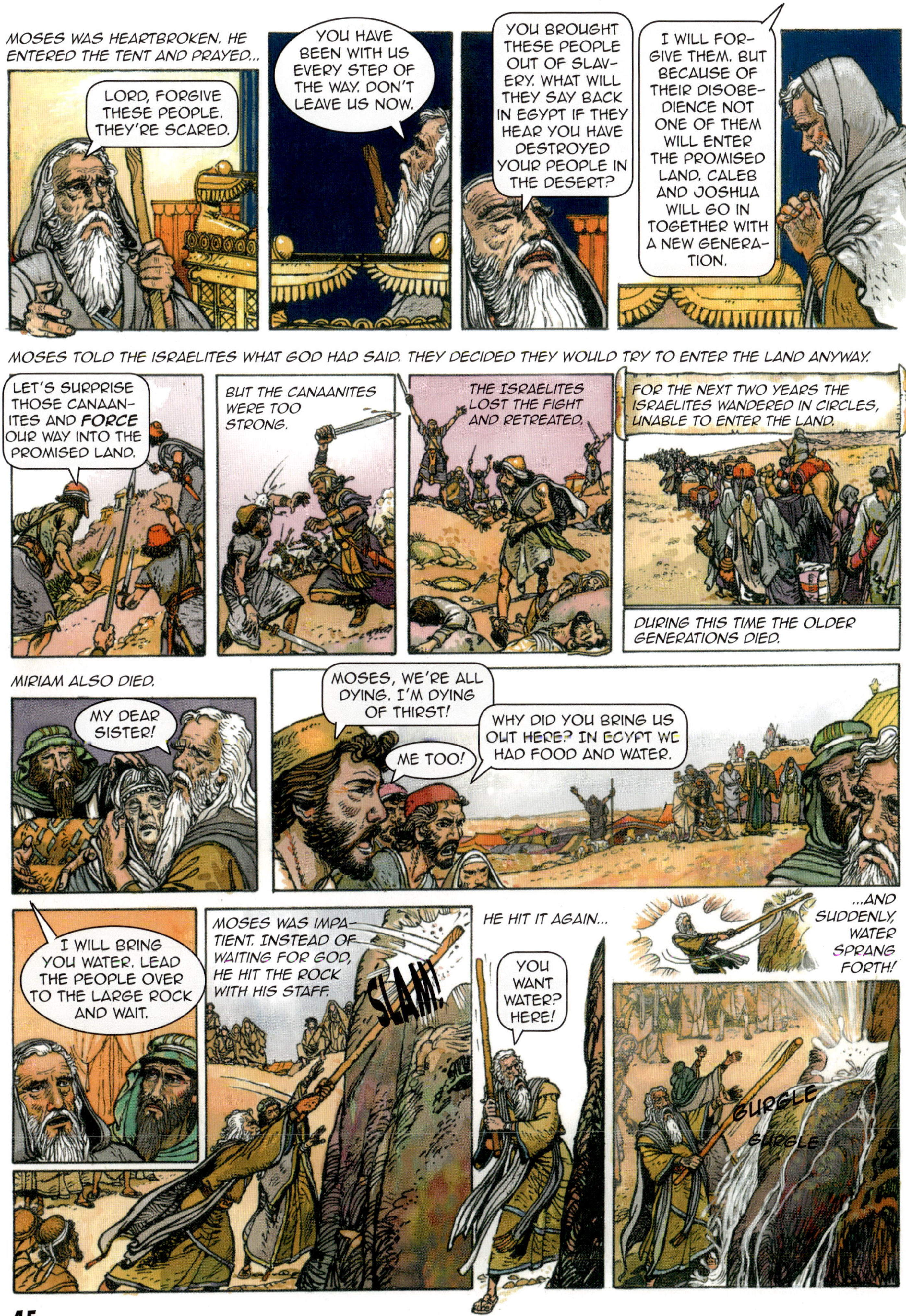

MOSES WAS HEARTBROKEN. HE ENTERED THE TENT AND PRAYED...
LORD, FORGIVE THESE PEOPLE. THEY'RE SCARED.
YOU HAVE BEEN WITH US EVERY STEP OF THE WAY. DON'T LEAVE US NOW.
YOU BROUGHT THESE PEOPLE OUT OF SLAVERY. WHAT WILL THEY SAY BACK IN EGYPT IF THEY HEAR YOU HAVE DESTROYED YOUR PEOPLE IN THE DESERT?
I WILL FORGIVE THEM. BUT BECAUSE OF THEIR DISOBEDIENCE NOT ONE OF THEM WILL ENTER THE PROMISED LAND. CALEB AND JOSHUA WILL GO IN TOGETHER WITH A NEW GENERATION.
MOSES TOLD THE ISRAELITES WHAT GOD HAD SAID. THEY DECIDED THEY WOULD TRY TO ENTER THE LAND ANYWAY.
LET'S SURPRISE THOSE CANAANITES AND **FORCE** OUR WAY INTO THE PROMISED LAND.
BUT THE CANAANITES WERE TOO STRONG.
THE ISRAELITES LOST THE FIGHT AND RETREATED.
FOR THE NEXT TWO YEARS THE ISRAELITES WANDERED IN CIRCLES, UNABLE TO ENTER THE LAND.
DURING THIS TIME THE OLDER GENERATIONS DIED.
MIRIAM ALSO DIED.
MY DEAR SISTER!
MOSES, WE'RE ALL DYING. I'M DYING OF THIRST!
ME TOO!
WHY DID YOU BRING US OUT HERE? IN EGYPT WE HAD FOOD AND WATER.
I WILL BRING YOU WATER. LEAD THE PEOPLE OVER TO THE LARGE ROCK AND WAIT.
MOSES WAS IMPATIENT. INSTEAD OF WAITING FOR GOD, HE HIT THE ROCK WITH HIS STAFF.
SLAM!
HE HIT IT AGAIN...
YOU WANT WATER? HERE!
...AND SUDDENLY, WATER SPRANG FORTH!
GURGLE
GURGLE

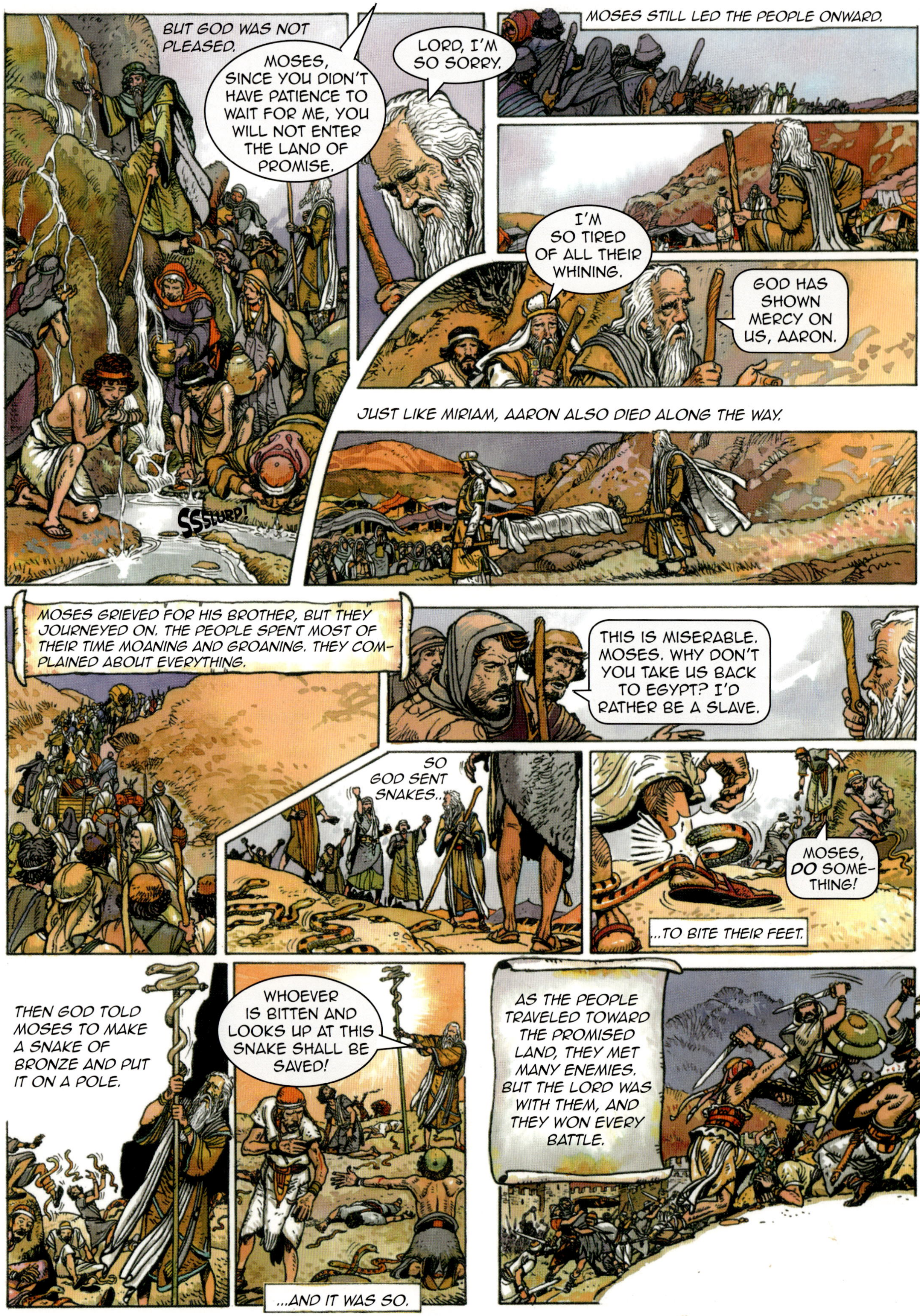
BUT GOD WAS NOT PLEASED.
MOSES, SINCE YOU DIDN'T HAVE PATIENCE TO WAIT FOR ME, YOU WILL NOT ENTER THE LAND OF PROMISE.
SSSLURP!
LORD, I'M SO SORRY.
MOSES STILL LED THE PEOPLE ONWARD.
I'M SO TIRED OF ALL THEIR WHINING.
GOD HAS SHOWN MERCY ON US, AARON.
JUST LIKE MIRIAM, AARON ALSO DIED ALONG THE WAY.
MOSES GRIEVED FOR HIS BROTHER, BUT THEY JOURNEYED ON. THE PEOPLE SPENT MOST OF THEIR TIME MOANING AND GROANING. THEY COMPLAINED ABOUT EVERYTHING.
THIS IS MISERABLE. MOSES. WHY DON'T YOU TAKE US BACK TO EGYPT? I'D RATHER BE A SLAVE.
SO GOD SENT SNAKES...
...TO BITE THEIR FEET.
MOSES, DO SOMETHING!
THEN GOD TOLD MOSES TO MAKE A SNAKE OF BRONZE AND PUT IT ON A POLE.
WHOEVER IS BITTEN AND LOOKS UP AT THIS SNAKE SHALL BE SAVED!
...AND IT WAS SO.
AS THE PEOPLE TRAVELED TOWARD THE PROMISED LAND, THEY MET MANY ENEMIES. BUT THE LORD WAS WITH THEM, AND THEY WON EVERY BATTLE.

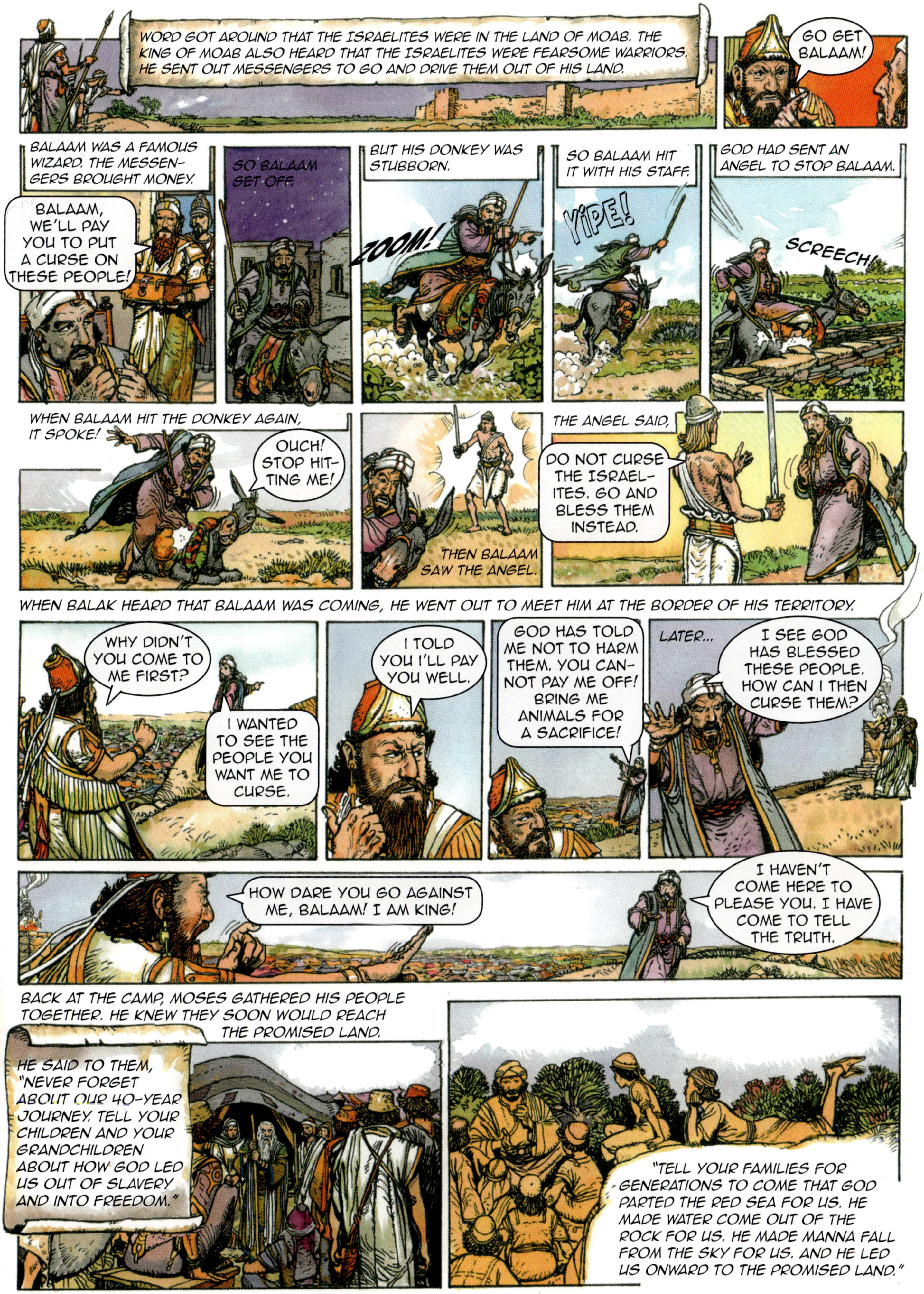
WORD GOT AROUND THAT THE ISRAELITES WERE IN THE LAND OF MOAB. THE KING OF MOAB ALSO HEARD THAT THE ISRAELITES WERE FEARSOME WARRIORS. HE SENT OUT MESSENGERS TO GO AND DRIVE THEM OUT OF HIS LAND.
GO GET BALAAM!
BALAAM WAS A FAMOUS WIZARD. THE MESSENGERS BROUGHT MONEY.
BALAAM, WE'LL PAY YOU TO PUT A CURSE ON THESE PEOPLE!
SO BALAAM SET OFF.
BUT HIS DONKEY WAS STUBBORN.
ZOOM!
SO BALAAM HIT IT WITH HIS STAFF.
YIPE!
GOD HAD SENT AN ANGEL TO STOP BALAAM.
SCREECH!
WHEN BALAAM HIT THE DONKEY AGAIN, IT SPOKE!
OUCH! STOP HITTING ME!
THEN BALAAM SAW THE ANGEL.
THE ANGEL SAID,
DO NOT CURSE THE ISRAELITES. GO AND BLESS THEM INSTEAD.
WHEN BALAK HEARD THAT BALAAM WAS COMING, HE WENT OUT TO MEET HIM AT THE BORDER OF HIS TERRITORY.
WHY DIDN'T YOU COME TO ME FIRST?
I WANTED TO SEE THE PEOPLE YOU WANT ME TO CURSE.
I TOLD YOU I'LL PAY YOU WELL.
GOD HAS TOLD ME NOT TO HARM THEM. YOU CANNOT PAY ME OFF! BRING ME ANIMALS FOR A SACRIFICE!
LATER...
I SEE GOD HAS BLESSED THESE PEOPLE. HOW CAN I THEN CURSE THEM?
HOW DARE YOU GO AGAINST ME, BALAAM! I AM KING!
I HAVEN'T COME HERE TO PLEASE YOU. I HAVE COME TO TELL THE TRUTH.
BACK AT THE CAMP, MOSES GATHERED HIS PEOPLE TOGETHER. HE KNEW THEY SOON WOULD REACH THE PROMISED LAND.
HE SAID TO THEM, "NEVER FORGET ABOUT OUR 40-YEAR JOURNEY. TELL YOUR CHILDREN AND YOUR GRANDCHILDREN ABOUT HOW GOD LED US OUT OF SLAVERY AND INTO FREEDOM."
"TELL YOUR FAMILIES FOR GENERATIONS TO COME THAT GOD PARTED THE RED SEA FOR US. HE MADE WATER COME OUT OF THE ROCK FOR US. HE MADE MANNA FALL FROM THE SKY FOR US. AND HE LED US ONWARD TO THE PROMISED LAND."

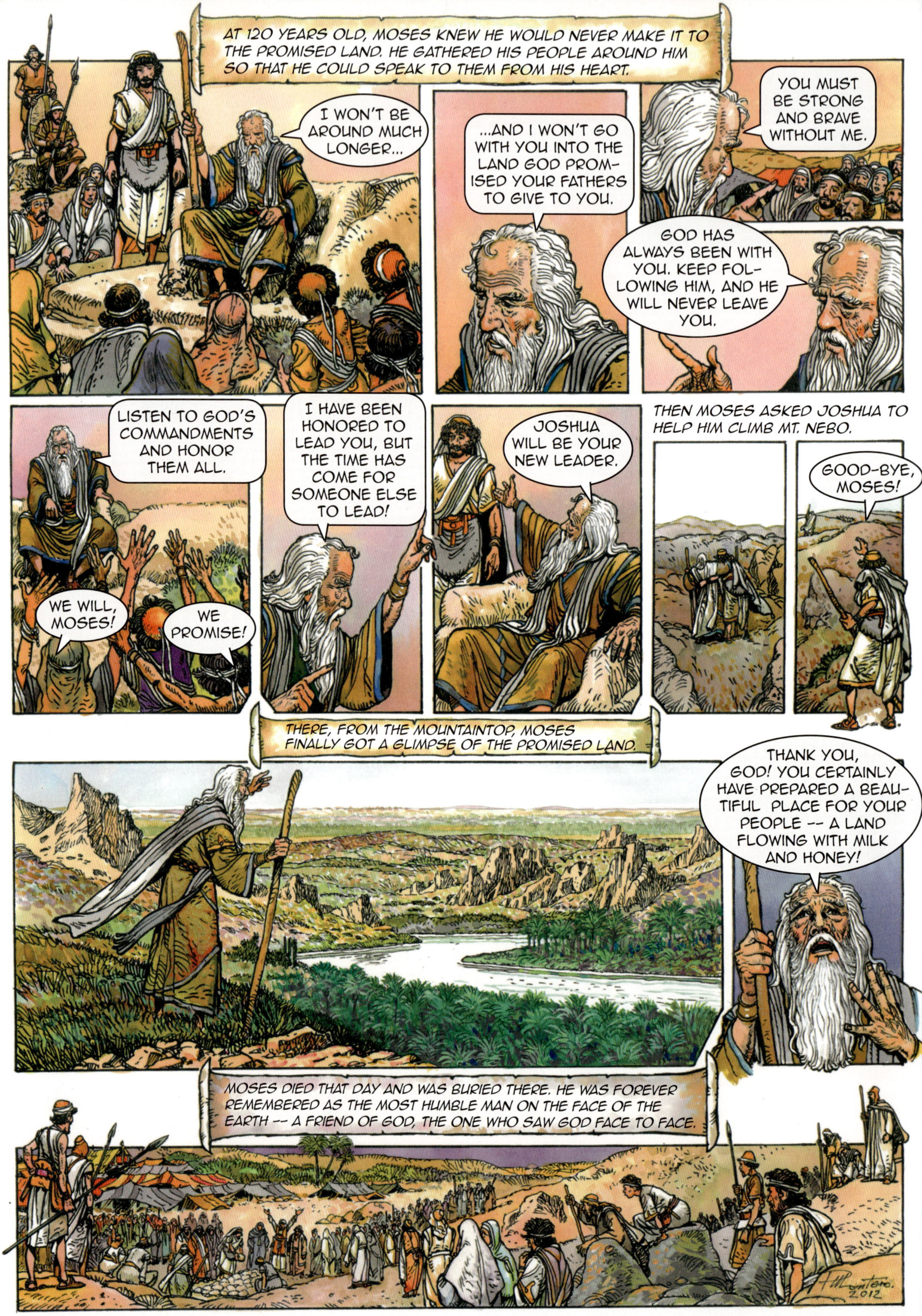
AT 120 YEARS OLD, MOSES KNEW HE WOULD NEVER MAKE IT TO THE PROMISED LAND. HE GATHERED HIS PEOPLE AROUND HIM SO THAT HE COULD SPEAK TO THEM FROM HIS HEART.
I WON'T BE AROUND MUCH LONGER...
...AND I WON'T GO WITH YOU INTO THE LAND GOD PROMISED YOUR FATHERS TO GIVE TO YOU.
YOU MUST BE STRONG AND BRAVE WITHOUT ME.
GOD HAS ALWAYS BEEN WITH YOU. KEEP FOLLOWING HIM, AND HE WILL NEVER LEAVE YOU.
LISTEN TO GOD'S COMMANDMENTS AND HONOR THEM ALL.
WE WILL, MOSES!
WE PROMISE!
I HAVE BEEN HONORED TO LEAD YOU, BUT THE TIME HAS COME FOR SOMEONE ELSE TO LEAD!
JOSHUA WILL BE YOUR NEW LEADER.
THEN MOSES ASKED JOSHUA TO HELP HIM CLIMB MT. NEBO.
GOOD-BYE, MOSES!
THERE, FROM THE MOUNTAINTOP, MOSES FINALLY GOT A GLIMPSE OF THE PROMISED LAND.
THANK YOU, GOD! YOU CERTAINLY HAVE PREPARED A BEAUTIFUL PLACE FOR YOUR PEOPLE -- A LAND FLOWING WITH MILK AND HONEY!
MOSES DIED THAT DAY AND WAS BURIED THERE. HE WAS FOREVER REMEMBERED AS THE MOST HUMBLE MAN ON THE FACE OF THE EARTH -- A FRIEND OF GOD, THE ONE WHO SAW GOD FACE TO FACE.
2012